James Walvin was born in Manchester. After graduating from the University of Keele, he did graduate work at McMaster University, Canada, before taking his doctorate at the University of York. Since 1967 he has taught at the University of York, where he is currently Reader in the History Department.

He has published widely on slave history and on British social history. Among his books are *A Child's World: A Social History of English Childhood 1800–1914*, *Passage to Britain*, *English Urban Life 1776–1851*, and *Black and White: The Negro and English Society 1555–1945*, which was awarded the Martin Luther King Memorial Prize for 1974. He was a historical adviser to the Granada Television series *Victorian Values*, to which the present book is a companion.

'Not a book to be read by anyone who would prefer their (and Mrs Thatcher's) myths to be left undisturbed'

INDEPENDENT

D1341244

JAMES WALVIN

VICTORIAN VALUES

CARDÍNAL

SPHERE BOOKS LTD

Published by the Penguin Group
27 Wrights Lane, London w8 5tz, England
Viking Penguin Inc., 40 West 23rd Street, New York, New York 10010, USA
Penguin Books Australia Ltd, Ringwood, Victoria, Australia
Penguin Books Canada Ltd, 2801 John Street, Markham, Ontario, Canada l3r 1b4
Penguin Books (NZ) Ltd, 182–190 Wairau Road, Auckland 10, New Zealand

Penguin Books Ltd, Registered Offices: Harmondsworth, Middlesex, England

First published in Great Britain by André Deutsch Ltd 1987
Published in Cardinal by Sphere Books Ltd 1988

Made and printed in Great Britain by
Richard Clay Ltd, Bungay, Suffolk

CONTENTS

ACKNOWLEDGEMENTS

In writing this book, I have been greatly helped by a number of people. My first debt is to my fellow historians, whose researches in diverse areas of nineteenth-century history provided the foundations for this study. Although their names are buried in the bibliography, it is only proper that I should recognise them, collectively, at the beginning of the book. Four people undertook the difficult task of typing from my hand-written drafts and I am delighted to thank Angela Bailey, Sue Parsons, Muriel Pirozek and June Rogers. I was given enormous help and encouragement by Maxine Baker and the team of the Granada Television series *Victorian Values* which was the starting point of this book. Celia Dougherty also rendered valuable assistance. Various ideas came from Byron Criddle, Phil Rees, Gavin Tate and Ben Benfield. The pictures were expertly assembled by Anne-Marie Ehrlich. John Parker improved the book by his expert scrutiny of the manuscript. Andrew Robinson and Anthony Thwaite proved to be exemplary editors, sparing neither my prose nor my feelings. Thanks also to Howard Davies, for his scrupulous copy-editing. I am immensely grateful to them and I hope they recognise that the book has been immeasurably improved by their detailed efforts.

The production team on *Victorian Values* was: Bamber Gascoigne (presenter), Maxine Baker (producer), Mick Gold (director), Kate Woods and Liz Andrew (researchers), Rod Caird (executive producer), Ian Jack (writer), Dr Bill Bynum, Professor Derek Fraser, Dr James Walvin (historical advisers).

J.W.
September 1986

LIST OF
ILLUSTRATIONS

CHRONOLOGY
1801–1901

1801	First census
1815	Battle of Waterloo; end of the French Wars
1819	Peterloo
	'Six Acts'
1829	*April* Catholic Emancipation
	September Metropolitan Police Act
1830–2	The reform crisis
1831–2	First cholera epidemic
1832	Passing of Reform Act
1833	Factory Act
1834	Poor Law Amendment Act
1835	Municipal Corporations Act
1837	*June* Accession of Victoria
1838–48	Chartist agitation
1840	*January* Penny post introduced
	February Victoria marries Prince Albert
1841	Peel Conservative Prime Minister
1844	Factory Act
1846	Repeal of Corn Laws
	Split of Conservative Party
1847	Ten Hour Act
1848	Revolutions in Europe
1848	Public Health Act
1851	Great Exhibition in Hyde Park
1854–5	Crimean War
1856	County and Borough Police Act; all counties and boroughs obliged to establish police force

1867	Second Reform Act
1868	*February* Disraeli Conservative Prime Minister
	December Gladstone Liberal Prime Minister
1869	Charity Organisation Society established
1870	Education Act (Foster's)
1874	Disraeli Prime Minister
1875	Artisans' Dwellings Act
1877	Victoria proclaimed Empress of India
1880	Gladstone Prime Minister
	Education Act; compulsory schooling
1885	Housing of the Working Classes Act
1886	Salisbury Conservative Prime Minister
1895	Salisbury returned as Conservative Prime Minister
1899	Boer War
1900	Formation of Labour Representation Committee (LRC)
1901	*January* Death of Victoria; accession of Edward VII

I

THE LAMENTING OF THINGS PAST

I was brought up to work jolly hard. We were taught to live within our income, that cleanliness is next to godliness. We were taught self-respect. You were taught tremendous pride in your country. All those are Victorian virtues . . .

Margaret Thatcher
(*The Standard*, April 1983)

TEACHERS of history often complain that it is difficult to interest their pupils in history. Pupils in their turn often describe history as boring or dull. When the Prime Minister of the United Kingdom gives her own history lessons, however, she commands attention and interest where others fail. Between 1983 and 1986 (and doubtless into the future) Margaret Thatcher and her senior supporting ministers periodically raised historical issues as major topics of contemporary political importance. From the alleged virtues of the nineteenth century and the much-denounced vices of the 'permissive society' of the 1960s, Conservative ministers have made a concerted attempt to store up a stock of contemporary political ammunition. There is of course nothing new in this, and certainly nothing unique to the Conservative Party. In Britain, all the major and fringe parties shape their proposals and their ideology in large part to a particular view of the past. All parties aim not simply to put to right the problems they see around them, but to alter the historical forces which have shaped and determined those problems. The Labour Party is more overt; its analysis of social ills points to the long-term defects of the capitalist order; but Conservatives have their own, generally less blatant view of history. However different their policies, both parties are nonetheless influenced to some degree by an historical outlook and by a determination to avoid the mistakes of the past or to maintain what they see as the inheritance of the past. At this level history is a political lumber room into which politicians discard outdated items or in which they rediscover forgotten and neglected treasures and memories.

History is, in a sense, the most democratic of forces, freely available to everyone. It does not belong to the professional historian but is available, as memory, folklore or legend, for people to make of it what they will. In fact the distinction between history and fiction is a relatively recent one. In classical writing, in medieval chronicles and in the nebulous world of the ballad, history as fact was often intermingled with history as imagination and fantasy. Since the Renaissance, however, historians have sought to distinguish their own work from that of others such as poets and novelists. The ground vacated by modern historians has been successfully occupied by historical novelists, from Scott and Dickens through to Catherine Cookson, who have proved immensely successful in purveying images of the fictional past. In the nineteenth and twentieth centuries, the historical novel reached, and reaches still, a far greater audience than any conventional work of historical scholarship. It is a matter of regret to many historians, but a fact nonetheless, that some of the most potent images of the past have sprung not from historical reality but from imagination. Consider the number of best-selling novels in English in recent years illustrating the point: *Schindler's Ark, Midnight's Children, Ragtime, The Color Purple, Roots.* There are millions of people whose knowledge of aspects of the past is derived in large part from such works of fiction, and from their film versions. Although historians remain uncomfortable with this fact, it is abundantly clear that history can be a potent force even when mythical or untrue.

When thinking of the recent past we are influenced by perhaps the most notoriously unreliable historical guide of all: memory. Historians have long been fascinated by the links between memory and history, though by and large they tend to minimise it as a reliable guide to the past. One of the many superficial attractions of the Victorian age is the fact that it is at once distant, in that only the very old can remember it, but also close enough for many of its memories and influences to linger on. Margaret Thatcher and her colleagues, born and reared in the 1920s and 1930s, clearly have no direct experience of Victorian life, but were surrounded by recollections of older relatives, friends, teachers and the like. Perhaps it is not surprising that they turned to the images of Victorian Britain in a conscious attempt to use 'the lessons of history' to their party advantage.

What happened in 1983 and after was quite different from the generally unconscious or implicit way politicians normally use the historical past. Two distinct historical epochs were singled out for praise and condemnation. The one, Victorian, which ran chronologically from 1837 to 1901; the other, the 'permissive society', its chronology confused, though its tone unmistakable, embracing the mid-1960s and early 1970s. The latter was (or so it is argued) the polar opposite of the former; the iconoclasm of the cultural revolution which then affected the western world was in large part a rejection of many of the values and norms lovingly created (and with such beneficial effect) by our forebears.

Of the two, however, it is the prominence given to Victorian society – to 'Victorian values' – which has caught the eye. The concept 'Victorian values' has entered the vernacular, repeated time and again by politicians and the media. The concept has excited fierce opposition, notably from historians on the left who have challenged the interpretation of Victorian history on which the concept depends. Such critics, however, face distinct difficulties. They argue that Margaret Thatcher has persuaded the public that the idea of Victorian values is an unassailable fact, a set of indisputable beliefs and virtues; whereas in fact the idea represents a particular, partial and debatable interpretation of nineteenth-century history. Yet such critics can never hope to command the attention or publicity given to Margaret Thatcher, and are unlikely to demolish her case effectively in the public eye. To make their problems worse, such critics tend to talk to themselves, publishing their views in journals of limited circulation which are read, in the main, by people never likely to accept Margaret Thatcher's views anyway.

To increase the difficulties for those keen to see the concept criticised, professional historians are reluctant to enter the debate. Many historians are loath even to argue the point, claiming, with some justice, that the very debate is spurious, in that it is, in the words of Michael Delahaye, 'impossible to abstract a single set of moral notions from a period that spanned sixty-three years'. This ought perhaps to be a spur to historians to say something. Instead, we are faced by that reluctance which stems from the slow-moving, restricted specialisation of the academic historian. There is an abundance of evidence available from which to shape a contrary argument, though much of it lies buried in specialist journals and

3

monographs. What follows is an attempt to draw on that work, to use the findings of many other people researching in the field, to shape a critical historical view of 'Victorian values'. The book is not *the* answer, but rather one of many possible answers. It is highly personal: I make no claim to do more than provide my own interpretation of 'Victorian values'. The past lends itself to an infinite variety of interpretations – a point which *itself* raises question marks against the concept of Victorian values. What follows is no more than one historian's reconstruction.

In the General Election of 1983 and in government thereafter Margaret Thatcher and other Cabinet ministers frequently returned to the question of Victorian values. Why they should do so, and why the appeal proved so successful, despite its patent flaws, are questions more for the political observer than the historian. The obvious answer is that the decision to adopt the concept was decided upon by that caucus of senior politicians, marketing agencies and media advisers which collectively conspires to create the issues and messages which are conveyed to the voting public. One of the attractions of looking towards Victorian history is that it seems to provide a sharp contrast to the current depressing state of Britain. Few could deny that late Victorian Britain was one of the world's leading powers, at the peak of economic and imperial achievement. Britannia not only ruled the waves but she ruled vast tracts of the globe's surface, and her industries – pioneering and (as it seemed) unmatched – dominated the markets of the world.

However flawed this image might be in detail, it is, in essence, an accurate picture of Britain at the time of Victoria's death. Britain had been unquestionably great at the turn of the century; why not aspire to a revival of that greatness? And where better to begin the necessary task of national revival than by invoking the personal values which seemed to lie behind Britain's pre-eminence in the nineteenth century? If late twentieth-century Britons could simply model themselves on the ideals and values of their Victorian forebears, the process of national rejuvenation could begin. This view of history struck a chord among many people who knew that Britain was once the world's major power. If the evocation of 'Victorian values' was banal and historically dubious, it was, for all that, an astute political ploy, which captured nostalgia for a better past and offered the illusory prospect of an improved future.

The real strength of the appeal to 'Victorian values' lay, and lies, not so much in an historical image but in the antidote it seems to offer to contemporary British ailments. It has become impossible, living in Britain in the 1970s and 1980s, to remain unaware of the arguments about the decline of Britain. There has grown up a specialised literature concerned solely with the history and process of decline. All major parties pledged themselves to reverse that decline. The topic is discussed regularly on TV, the radio and in the press. In the form of massive economic contraction, industrial collapse and unemployment, the personal consequences of the decline directly affect millions of people. The British have come to accept that their country has suffered, and continues to suffer, a slide from economic and global power.

The explanations for that slide are greatly disputed by economists and politicians, whatever their outlook, who invariably incorporate a major historical theme in their particular analysis. Indeed the arguments have in large part been historical arguments. The alleged source of the nation's decline varies greatly: trade unions, management, education, the City, Parliament – each has been blamed by someone for causing or adding to the nation's deterioration. But all point to history as the key and determining context. Indeed there have been many commentators who interpreted the decline as a specifically historical phenomenon. In the words of the Hudson Report (1974):

> Britain in the 1970s is very largely a creation of the mid-Victorian period ... Many of the country's problems are Victorian problems or stem from attempts to operate Victorian solutions in a society that exists in a late twentieth-century world. In a nutshell, Victorian Britain attempted to come to terms with a crude industrialism; the Britain of the 1970s has refused to look beyond it.

This, a more overt historical explanation than most, manages to capture the essential point – that Britain's present and future decline has grown from Victorian roots. Furthermore, this is an assumption shared by students of decline from all political quarters; left, right and centre point their accusing fingers at the late nineteenth century. Some critics have argued that even by the turn of the century cracks had begun to reveal themselves in Britain's economic edifice. The industrial lead was challenged by Germany and the USA; trade was looked down upon and manufacturing held in low esteem among the wealthy; public schools and universities failed to address the nation's major needs; the empire soaked up too much British talent; amateurism prevailed over professionalism in a range of British institutions.

It is true that many observers looked to more recent developments for their explanations of decline, to the growth of trade union power or to the stifling bureaucracy of the Welfare State. Yet it is quite impossible to understand both these phenomena if they are wrenched free from the nineteenth century, for both originated and grew in response to Victorian problems. Whichever approach the critic adopted, it was virtually impossible to avoid confronting aspects of Victorian society. It is, then, an extraordinary turn of events to find, in the midst of this continuing debate, that the very society blamed for the nation's predicament has been singled out as a model of virtue, one whose prime qualities we should all re-adopt.

The simple explanation would be that in the world of party political conflict, and especially in General Elections, politicians do not always mean precisely what they say. It would be easier to let such slips pass away unnoticed and unremarked. The problem is that the evocation of 'Victorian values' has succeeded in intruding the idea deep into contemporary popular usage. Despite the concept's contentiousness, despite the conflict with many explanations of British decline, the term 'Victorian values' continues to roll easily from the tongue. It is an idea which has the virtue of defying easy definition, yet people have no trouble knowing exactly what it means. It is a concept which has been divorced from its historical roots, representing instead a simple code of good behaviour and decent ideals. But the concept hinges upon a view of the past which is debatable. This book is written as a contribution to that debate.

2

ALL SORTS
AND CONDITIONS

THE PEOPLE OF
VICTORIAN BRITAIN

THE transformations in British society in the course of the
nineteenth century were extraordinary and profound. But of all
those changes, few seemed more remarkable – to contemporaries
and, later, to historians – than the relentless rise in population.
Today, when we are accustomed to thinking of Britain as an
overcrowded island, it is easy to overlook the fact that this is a
relatively recent phenomenon. When the first modern census was
taken in 1801 it revealed a population of some 10½ million for
England, Scotland and Wales. By 1851, the year of the Great
Exhibition, the people of Britain numbered 21 million. At the time
of Victoria's death in 1901, the number of her British people had
grown to 37 million. In the course of Victoria's reign (1837–1901)
her people had doubled in numbers, from approximately 18½
million to 37 million. It is true of course that similar population
growth was to be found throughout Western Europe and North
America in those same years – with the disastrous exception of
Ireland. In Britain, the rate of growth, measured each decade,
remained high between 1787 and 1911. In that period the population grew by more than 10 per cent each decade. The causes of such
growth need not detain us here. But the consequences of population increase are central not only to any reconstruction of
nineteenth-century history but also, and particularly, to the concern of this book. Indeed our very perception of Victorian society is
shaped in large part by the human and social consequences of
population growth.

What made the increase in population so obvious, and unavoidable, was the shift in the centre of gravity of the British people. In

the course of the nineteenth century the British – but especially the English – became a nation of town dwellers. In the late seventeenth century, perhaps 25 per cent of the English people lived in urban areas – all of which, with the exception of London, were small by modern standards. By the time of the first census this had risen to a third and by the mid-nineteenth century, to more than 50 per cent. If, technically, the British people had become an urban nation by mid-century, most of them lived in small towns, rather than major cities. Not until the late century did the great majority of the nation, some three-quarters, live in towns and cities.

At Victoria's death more than half the nation's town dwellers – some 14,200,000 – were to be found in towns and cities containing more than 100,000 people. By then, the concept of the 'conurbation' was introduced to describe the nation's six massive urban areas: London, South-East Lancashire, the West Midlands, West Yorkshire, Merseyside and Tyneside. Put in its simplest form, at the time of Victoria's accession, a minority of her people were town dwellers; at her death the overwhelming majority lived in a major urban area. What to do with this rapidly growing and urbanising people – how to feed, house, wash, treat, educate, control and care for them – were problems at the heart of Victorian politics and thought.

Writers, from home and abroad, painters, and observers of all persuasions made frequent and startled comments on the rapid and uncontrolled growth of British cities and towns. For much of the nineteenth century, the city was synonymous with dirt, disease, overcrowding, smells and noise. It is true that this had always been the case – as true of seventeenth-century London (as any reader of Pepys can attest) as it was of nineteenth-century Manchester. But what made the Victorian cities worse was their massive and ever-increasing size, their noxious and noisy industries, and the density of their population.

Towns and cities were, above all else, killers of their inhabitants, though this may seem a bizarre point to make in the context of a growing population. It was often the case that there were more deaths than births in the towns, and that the growth of population was often made possible only by migration into the area.

Towns which had once been insignificant – or even non-existent – rapidly became major cities familiar to the modern reader. Before the nineteenth century, the major 'provincial capitals' had been Norwich, Bristol, York, Exeter and Newcastle, though London was twenty times the size of its nearest rival. But the 'new

HAULING CART IN PIT-PASSAGE, 1842

SALVATION ARMY SHELTER FOR WOMEN, WHITECHAPEL, 1892

WENTWORTH STREET, WHITECHAPEL, BY DORÉ

118 High Street, Glasgow, 1868

towns', especially in the Midlands and the North, soon relegated most of the old provincial towns to economic and demographic insignificance. By 1851 the seven largest towns in England and Wales, excluding London, were Liverpool, Manchester, Birmingham, Bristol, Leeds, Sheffield and Bradford. Yet, odd as it may seem, the towns which had the greatest growth were not industrial towns or ports, but resort towns, dotted around the coastline and providing day-trippers and holiday-makers with a pleasurable and healthy escape from the grime and dangers of the inland industrial and urban areas. We need to remember that Blackpool no less than Birmingham was primarily a nineteenth-century town, given its modern being and rationale by the economic and social needs of the British people.

The British people not only increased in numbers, year by year, but they were remarkable travellers and migrants. As we have seen, the towns and cities soaked up armies of migrant peoples, normally travelling short distances in the first instance, to find work, shelter, friendship or merely the dim prospects of work, food or better times than were to be had in their bleak rural homes. Country girls seeking servants' posts, young men in search of casual work created by many new industries (notably in London) – these formed the main columns of a migrating army of people which marched the length of Britain throughout these years. In times of industrial buoyancy or agricultural depression, the numbers were swelled by the ranks of the desperate. In the ten years 1841–51 one-third of a million immigrants settled in London, traditionally the home of tens of thousands of 'outsiders'. Few were more noticeable than the Irish, who became a by-word for wretched poverty and who, in the famine years of the 1840s died or fled Ireland in their millions. In 1851 more than 109,000 Irish-born lived in London. At the most wretched of times, the 1840s, thousands of Irish landed in Liverpool every year. And even late in the century a regular flow of Irish people continued to cross the Irish Sea to British cities. But the Irish were only the most obvious and numerous of settlers. Scots and Welsh, as well as provincial English, had long been familiar groups in a number of English cities. Jews, a notable group in the capital since the seventeenth century, were joined by East European Jewish refugees after 1881. Between 1881 and 1914 upwards of 150,000 settled in Leeds, Manchester, Liverpool, Glasgow and above all in the East End of London. In 1901 31 per cent of Whitechapel's population was alien. There were other striking minorities, notably of Chinese and of

Indians, by the late century – most a direct result of the expansion of empire and of maritime trading ties to the outside world. But, on the whole, non-white faces were rare, a fact which in some degree explains the curiosity and amusement displayed towards visiting exotic foreigners in circus displays or at moments of imperial celebration.

The great bulk of migration took place within the British Isles, as individuals and families quit their birth-place, normally at a young age, to seek a better life in town or city. Of course many British migrated overseas, to the great benefit of white colonies and settlements around the world, notably to North America, South Africa and Australasia. In the seventy-seven years to 1851 some 845,000 people left Britain for settlement abroad; in the forty years to 1911 more than 1⅓ million Britons migrated overseas. But internal migration was even more striking. Throughout much of the period 1850–1900, towns absorbed at least half a million people per decade, a movement greatly assisted by the rapid spread of the modern railway system. Thus the human aggregate of British towns was made up of peoples drawn from the length and breadth of the British Isles. Although local city fathers sought to cultivate a civic pride and an attachment to the locality, the inhabitants of British towns and cities often owed their parochial and family allegiances to other, distant or rural communities.

For the great majority of the British people life remained at the end of our period what it had been for their ancestors – hard and unrewarding. In the course of that century it is true that many of the material benefits disgorged by the expanding industrial system, and by international trade, percolated down the social scale. But for all the industrial wealth of a notable minority, and notwithstanding the material and cultural confidence of the middle classes, for the great bulk of the British people life was a struggle. Historians continue to argue about the extent of the benefits that came the way of ordinary people as the century advanced – in wages, in housing, the necessities and the pleasures of life. But the limits of those gains cannot be denied.

Britain had, since the early century, established itself as the leading industrial nation of the world. For the first two generations, the benefits of that industrialisation seemed marginal, and in many cases brought more problems and disadvantages than rewards. Oddly enough, many of the occupations of Victorian people remained traditional and not always directly related to what we imagine to be industrialisation. The working population in 1881 stood at 11,200,000, with twice as many males as women working (formally at least). But in many key areas women predominated. In textiles, clothing manufacture and domestic service women outnumbered men; there were for instance 1,488,000 female compared to 196,000 male servants. Indeed domestic service was the largest single form of employment; agricultural work accounted for 1,436,000. In all the great variety of manufacturing jobs, 3,358,000 were employed, an indication of the new-found importance of British manufacturing industries. By Victoria's death in 1901 the situation had changed. Servants numbered almost two million, agriculture employed 1,192,000 and manufacture provided work for 4,139,000. Mining, building and transport had also increased its numbers but perhaps the most noticeable change was the growth in middle and lower middle class posts: in banking, insurance, the professions and public service. It was in these years that the new retail outlets and chains began to make their presence felt in the high street – a reflection of the fact that in these years 'more people had more to spend for a longer part of their lives than they had ever had before'. Shops owned by Liptons, Boots, Lever and the Co-op became architectural features of the British town. So too did the confusion of advertisements, hoardings and bill-posting on all available surfaces, announcing the consumer goods of the new industries: Rowntree's and Cadbury's chocolate, Huntley and Palmer's and McVitie's biscuits, Crosfield's and Pear's soap or Will's tobacco. In the provision of the nation's food and clothing, and – revealingly – of people's luxuries and pleasures (holidays, reading matter, smoking materials, transport and new mass entertainment), there developed new forms of economic activity. And, of course, each provided employment for growing numbers of people. By the end of the century there were major manufacturing, service and distributive industries designed to feed, shelter, clothe and entertain the British people in a totally new fashion and style. It seems clear in retrospect that the way of life of millions of late Victorians had changed more fundamentally than in any comparable era. Life in 1900 had made a qualitative shift from that available to Britons in the early years of Victoria's reign.

Much of this change was related to real wages which, despite occasional or local exceptions, showed a remarkable 80 per cent rise between 1850 and 1914. In the last quarter of the nineteenth century wholesale prices fell substantially, with the result that many basic foodstuffs, much of which came from the granaries of the New World or the livestock and dairies of Australasia, fell in price. Although an over-simplification it is true to claim that rising wages and falling prices proved a boon for the late Victorian consumer. The reverse side to this story, however, was that many businessmen complained of a slowing down in business, while agriculture undoubtedly passed through extremely difficult years. This fact continued to drive people from the land and into the towns or abroad, thus further compounding the rapid development of an urban society.

This image of general material improvement for the great bulk of the population by the end of Victoria's reign is, however, deceptive. It screened layers of deprivation and distress which continued to shock and outrage contemporaries, who were themselves more hardened to such experiences than we might be. Year after year, revelations appeared in the press, in Parliament or in book form cataloguing the continuing and apparently endless sufferings of major sections of the British people. In the year of Victoria's death, the young Winston Churchill was appalled by the revelations in Rowntree's classic study of poverty in York: 'I see little glory in an Empire which can rule the waves and is unable to flush its sewers.' Churchill was disturbed to read that the poor 'have only the workhouse or prison as the only avenues to change from their present situation'. Rowntree's survey revealed that almost three in ten of York's population were poor, 'underfed, ill-clothed and badly-housed'. Of all the local poor, one-third had income too low to meet even the most basic of physical needs, and three-quarters of extreme poverty was a result of low earnings – too low to provide for dependants and family. Moreover, it was perfectly clear that the majority of working people endured such poverty at some point in their life. How are we to reconcile this evidence with the alternative and conflicting image of improvement and material betterment?

In simple terms, there is nothing contradictory here. Material improvement came the way of many people, eluded many completely, and often came, but later disappeared, for others. Moreover, expectations continued to rise – a fact which simply accentuated the wretchedness of those unable to enjoy, or were deprived of, the better things in contemporary life. Even for those working people able to benefit from the improvements in food, clothing, housing and pleasures, these benefits were often fleeting and always hard-won. The widespread and abject exploitation of the first phase of industrial growth undoubtedly receded in the second half of the century. But this did not mean the end of those seemingly endemic problems of British labouring life: hard work, excessive hours, low pay, poor working conditions and a myriad of associated problems – notably ill-health and communal disease. In agriculture and in the new textile industries (the engine of the first industrial revolution), families formed the backbone of the labour force. This had always been true of most traditional plebeian labour. But the new industrial systems (before 1850) ensured a marked accentuation in the exploitation of women and young children, at a time when changing sensibilities and attitudes began to question the wisdom and morality of such behaviour. Hours were long and, despite increasing legislation, often uncontrolled or unchecked. If the 1833 Factory Act limited children's hours to eight per day, those aged 14 to 18 were allowed to work twelve. And even though the ten-hour day was established in 1847, not until 1878 was that norm extended to all factories and workshops. Nor did the coming of compulsory schooling in the 1880s end extensive child labour. In 1908 200,000 worked outside school hours. In the 'sweated trades' and workshops, especially in London and the Midlands, armies of children were to be found toiling away throughout their childhood, making hairpins, safety-pins, buttons, hooks and eyes, or engaged in any number of simple and ill-paid tasks. In 1905 Robert Sherrard found in a Birmingham slum

> three little children, busy at work at a table on which were heaped up piles of cards, and a vast mass of tangled hooks and eyes. The eldest girl was eleven, the next was nine, and a little boy of five completed the companionship. They were all working as fast as their little fingers could work.

In fact, such labour was made more commonplace by the development of new, lighter consumer industries. And, of course, child labour in agriculture remained ubiquitous. Even after the introduction of compulsory schooling in 1880, children were still withdrawn from school to work with their families, whenever the local harvest began.

Not only was the working week long, and for many unregulated either by unions or legislation, but the working life began at an early age and continued as long as physique or circumstances allowed. Protection through union activity failed, by and large, before 1850. Thereafter, and especially after 1880, trade unions began to make an impact in British life, gathering to themselves ever more members for whom they sought to secure better conditions of work and supporting legislative agreement. But even this was limited. Union membership in 1885 was available to only

10 per cent of the male labour force; by 1900 it had risen to 2 million, though much of that figure was represented by men in a few well-organised industries – mining, metals and transport for example.

In contrast to these 2 million unionists there were, for instance, 2 million domestic servants in what was, by any criterion, one of the most exploitative, ill-paid yet utterly unorganised occupations in Victorian life. Similarly, agricultural labourers – almost 1½ million as late as 1911 – were notoriously ill-paid, hard-worked, and practically impossible to organise into unions. Notwithstanding the undisputed evidence of increases and improvements in wages, the proliferation of more and more varied foods and material goods, and the occasional plebeian pleasure, in pub, holiday, sports stadium or seaside resort, the lives of late Victorian working people remained harsh. Moreover the difficulties of their lives made a telling contrast to the more lavish benefits enjoyed by their middle and upper class contemporaries.

At Victoria's death, the middle and upper classes numbered almost four million (some ten million fewer than the working class) and they were more numerous and more prosperous than ever before. Significantly they came to be known as the 'servant-keeping class'. Some of this class had worked their way up from humble positions. At the very top, the number of millionaires increased, the majority deriving their wealth from business or finance.

It is when we consider the working-class life cycle that we begin to understand why, in the midst of rising standards, hardship remained an inescapable feature of plebeian life. Unless a man or family was able to save substantial sums, his new-won security could be swept away by the accidents of fate and circumstance. It is true that working people did begin to save, in Friendly Societies, factory schemes, later in the savings banks, but their funds were generally inadequate to cope with life's emergencies or disasters. Illness or accident to the breadwinner, the death of a spouse, unemployment or large numbers of children, old age – all of these could plunge a family into the most distressing circumstances. Indeed in the course of a long lifetime it was inevitable that working people would endure most if not all of these problems. And to round off a lifetime's toil there followed the inescapable penury of old age. It was no accident that the largest single group to be found in the workhouses were the old. Indeed the largest single group of paupers at the end of Victoria's reign as at the

HOUNDSDITCH, LONDON, 1872, BY DORE

VICTORIA MILL, CLAYTON-LE-MOORS, NEAR MANCHESTER

SOCIETY OF FRIENDS SOUP KITCHEN, BALL STREET, MANCHESTER, 1862

WIGAN PIT WOMEN, BY MUNBY, 1865

HOUSES AND RAILWAY VIADUCT, BY DORE

beginning was the old; the next largest group was that of children. The continuing and nationwide poverty of the old is a timely reminder of how limited still were the material improvements of the late nineteenth century. It is indicative too of the constraints which still existed to working-class acquisitiveness and accumulation; even now few could adequately provide for themselves into the non-working days of old age. Something more was required than the workhouse, philanthropy or modest wages and regular employment. It was the realisation of this central fact which inspired the determination to secure adequate pensions for the old.

While few could save from their wages to safeguard their years of retirement, there were many whose wages were totally inadequate to maintain a decent standard of life even when in work. This was, as we have seen, one of the most startling discoveries of Seebohm Rowntree in York. But it had long been clear from a number of sources. The question of how to cope with the poor was not of course new. Few things had troubled the reign of Elizabeth I more than the difficulties posed by the poor. The rise in population in the eighteenth century and the consequences of the extensive wars with France created new dimensions to the problem, leading in 1795 to the 'Speenhamland System', where inadequate local wages were 'topped up' by an allowance based on the price of bread. This was a system which was fiercely criticised and replaced in 1834 by the Poor Law and its workhouses. Despite the criticisms of 1795, we need to consider the aim of Speenhamland. In tackling inadequate wages it sought to minimise an economic problem – low wages – which remained endemic throughout Victorian life. Throughout these years – and into the twentieth century – poverty haunted British life not simply because of personal fecklessness or lack of foresight, not merely because of the obvious traumas of unemployment, illness or old age, but for the basic reason that legions of British people were inadequately rewarded for their labours.

In a sense the poor were inescapable long before the massive surveys of Charles Booth in London (1889) and Rowntree in York (1901). Indeed the social and political struggle, both locally and centrally, to deal with the poor provides one of the most striking issues of British history throughout the period. The poor had, without doubt, always been with us, but rarely on such a scale and never in such ubiquitous and concentrated urban form. It is not to minimise agricultural poverty, itself persistent and unshifting, to point out that what made the poverty of Victorian life so different – in a sense so new – was its urban setting.

At the end, as at the beginning of the period, the poor constituted a major slice of British life. But by 1901 their problems were more conspicuous by virtue of their concentration in towns and cities. Booth's survey of East London found that the poor comprised some 30 per cent of the population. Rowntree confirmed this figure in his later study of York (though he had not expected to). This evidence was startling enough; even so poverty was almost certainly more extensive at mid-century and had begun to decline from the 1870s onwards.

Throughout the nineteenth century, the period was punctuated by debates about poverty; by revelations, surveys, legislation and political controversy generated by this, perhaps the most timeless of problems. At the worst of times, in the 'Hungry Forties' or in the turbulent late 1880s for example, it seemed to many that the tensions generated by poverty would tear apart the fabric of British life. Poverty seemed to be the breeding ground for those radical upsurges – Chartism in the 1840s, trade unionism and socialism in the 1880s – which became so testing a feature of British life. Paradoxically, however, concern about poverty reached a peak in the years 1889–1901, and up to World War I, at a time when poverty itself, according to the evidence, was less widespread than in earlier decades. Two factors might explain this. Firstly, the pace of urbanisation increased towards the end of the century and the problems of town and city life were more obvious to view. Secondly, attitudes towards poverty and other social issues were changing quite markedly. Put at its simplest, there was a new sensitivity abroad which was offended by, and sought remedies for, the grimmer aspects of urban life. There was, too, fear for the nation's future; how could so expansive and successful an industrial and imperial nation be at peace with itself when troubled by such levels of urban poverty? The Poor Law of 1834 – bitterly resisted by the poor themselves, for it consigned them to the new, inhuman workhouses – yielded interesting data about the poor. In 1834 1¼ million people received poor relief; by 1850 this had fallen to 1 million. But at the same time it was known that 2¼ million people had no gainful employment. The truth of the matter remained that, at mid-century, the real depths of poverty had scarcely been plumbed. Though there was a host of revealing studies, most strikingly Henry Mayhew's *London Labour and the London Poor* in the 1840s and 50s, not until Booth and Rowntree was the enormity of the problem confirmed by irrefutable statistical evidence, or even given an acceptable definition.

Given the extent of poverty throughout Victorian society, it is perhaps unusual that contemporaries should, periodically, be shocked by the latest revelation. To many Victorians the poor were distant and often unknown. They were, said Mayhew, 'a large body of persons of whom the public had less knowledge than the most distant tribes of the earth'. Thus it was that the latest findings shocked Victorians, prompting them anew to try to tackle the problem. This was as true of the response to Mayhew's work at mid-century as of Churchill's response to Rowntree in 1901. What made it possible, in between times, for Victorians to forget about or overlook the poverty close to home was the segregated social 'zoning' of many British cities. There was often a physical distance and barrier between the poor and the better-off. Poverty in its worst, concentrated forms was often to be found in the inaccessible quarters and courtyards of urban life. It was from these urban recesses that the social investigators were able to pry out the devastating evidence they laid before the Victorian public. Of course there were now, in an industralising world, new forms of poverty. When a highly specialised town, dependent on textiles, mining, metals, or whatever, found itself without work, the extent of local suffering was terrible. In Oldham during the textile crisis of 1847 some 41 per cent of people were in dire poverty. It was this form of localised poverty, the result of crisis in local industry, which was to plague Britain thereafter.

The consequences of poverty were far-reaching, not simply for the poor but also for society at large. Pregnant women, small children and developing adolescents were particularly prey to its problems. Indeed Rowntree's work underlined the point illustrated in other sources, that the physique and health of working people, especially the poorer classes, were greatly inferior to that of their social betters. The physical well-being of the nation had become a matter of great concern in the last twenty years of the century. The establishment of compulsory schooling had brought the nation's young into the classroom, and with them their illnesses, deformities and weaknesses. Indeed the ailments of the nation's young provided yet another shock for those worried about the nation's future. Large numbers suffered from poor eyesight, defective hearing, appalling dental problems and general lack of personal cleanliness. A similar picture emerged in the Boer War when only two out of five volunteers were considered fit for military service. Major-General Sir Frederick Maurice thought that one major cause was 'the continuous rush of the people from country districts into the towns . . .' In Manchester, of the 11,000 volunteers in 1899–1900, '8,000 were found to be physically unfit to carry a rifle and stand the fatigue of discipline'. The resulting parliamentary Committee on Physical Deterioration found 'very abundant signs of physical defect traceable to neglect, poverty and ignorance'. The intellectual climate of the years 1890–1914 made such evidence even more alarming. The rapid spread of the new 'science' of eugenics and heredity raised questions about whether the British 'race' was in the process of degeneration and decline.

Whatever the answer, the alarms such studies created took the worried observer back to the basic issue of urban deprivation and poverty. For those late Victorians (Lloyd George and Churchill are classic illustrations) concerned about the state and the future of Britain, it was the face of the urban poor which proved the most worrying of all contemporary issues. It came, too, at a time of increasing competition in industry and empire, from newer expansionist nations, notably the Germans and the Americans. In a world economy and a global grab for empire, and where only the fittest seemed to survive (or at least triumph), British poverty seemed a debilitating and divisive force. It blighted its victims, afflicted their descendants and seriously undermined the human foundations of economic success at home and abroad.

This was a miserable image to set alongside those colourful scenes of imperial celebration, the late-century royal jubilees when the greatest empire the world had seen paraded its manpower and its subject peoples, in all their native finery, through the streets of London. The fact was that only yards away from the routes of those majestic processions were to be found scenes of human squalor and suffering which raised serious questions about the whole conduct and direction of British social and political life. What was to be done, to use Churchill's words, about an empire which ruled the waves but could not flush its own sewers? One simple answer – and one reached by people of greatly differing political persuasions, from early socialists to the staunchest of conservatives – was to use the power of the state. But where to start when confronted by the manifold social problems obvious at the death of Victoria? Odd as it may seem, great improvements had taken place in her reign, which we shall now examine.

3

SICKNESS AND HEALTH

THE rapid growth in population in the early nineteenth century was once thought to be related to improvements in medicine. Historians now dismiss that argument. With the exception of a few infectious diseases, medicine had little impact on the overall health of the British people until well into Victoria's reign. Before 1820 there were, it is true, new hospitals in a number of bigger towns but few people were treated in them and there is little evidence that hospitals improved patients' chances of recovery or survival. The vast bulk of the population lived out their lives generally untouched by formal medicine throughout the first half of Victoria's reign. In fact it seems paradoxical, but as the British population grew in size, it appeared, to contemporary observers, to contain vast numbers of sick and weakly people. Not only were the British people notable for their levels of poverty, equally striking was the ubiquity of their major ailments. From the first there seemed to be a close correlation between poverty and sickness. And as Britain became ever more urbanised, these two related factors – poverty and disease – were seen to be inextricably linked to the urban habitat. The British people seemed to become collectively more sickly as they became a nation of town-dwellers. By the time of Victoria's death, and the disturbing evidence revealed by army recruitment, there was no longer any doubt that city life was the cause of many of the nation's physical problems.

This is not to claim however that widespread disease was peculiar to town life, or that it was new. Levels of disease in the pre-industrial world had been much worse, and the population kept in check by the periodic visitations of devastating plagues. Life in rural society was likewise unhealthy and disease-ridden, though rarely on the scale of the major cities. But the proliferation of major urban areas – all of them unplanned, filthy and noisome to live and work in – accentuated older, traditional patterns of urban disease, and then became the breeding ground for new ones. Throughout Victorian Britain, a host of diseases regularly killed large numbers of Britons and left large numbers of survivors with life-long troublesome afflictions.

The dangers began at birth, for infant – and child – mortality was in some respects the most serious of physical obstacles. Moreover, for certain sections of the population, levels of infant mortality were worse at the end of the century than they had been at the beginning. In 1839–40 the death rate for babies was 153 per thousand, in 1896 it stood at 156, and by 1899 it had risen to 163. In 1975 it was only 17.5. There were, of course, variations in these patterns but whichever town historians have studied, the overall impression is the same. In York for instance between 1834 and 1842, 42 per cent of all recorded deaths were of children under the age of 5. Perhaps even more striking were the differences between the social classes. In mid-century Bath one working-class child in two died before the age of 5, whilst in middle-class homes only one child in eleven. At the end of the century, in the worst areas of Liverpool, the level of infant mortality was a staggering 509 per thousand. Rowntree was appalled by the parallel evidence he unearthed in York. 'When we examine the mortality of children under twelve months of age, we find the same terrible waste of human life proceeding in the poorer areas.' There were, by 1899, striking improvements in medicine and medical care, but these improvements had scarcely begun to make an impression on the nation's levels of infant mortality. Such figures can only hint at the continuing depths of pain and suffering of parents and family, confronted by the regularity of infant deaths in their midst.

For working people, few things seemed more likely than the loss of a baby or child – a fact which explains the continuing need to insure for death and burial, through Friendly Societies and Burial Clubs. The loss of babies and children, so commonplace among Victorians, is perhaps one of the greatest divides between ourselves and our ancestors. Victorian children succumbed to a host of ailments which, though lethal to people of all age groups, were especially dangerous for the young. Measles, for instance, never killed fewer than 7,000 people annually in the nineteenth century. Whooping cough was calculated to have killed two-fifths of all children under 5. Scarlet fever had its most deadly impact on the age group 4–8. And tuberculosis, though gradually declining as the century advanced, remained the worst of British urban killers.

Among the surviving children, disease and illness often left them disabled or afflicted to some degree. Moreover the appalling domestic environment and the even worse working conditions endured by millions of children, working in their formative years in polluted atmospheres, invariably had a disastrous effect on children's health. The horror stories of child labour in the years of early industries have become part of British folklore (and are nonetheless true for all that). But similar evidence continued to emerge throughout the century in a host of new smaller scale occupations employing children. The sweatshops, cottage industries, rural employments of the mid and late century continued to make their own distinctive ravages on the health of their young employees. Stunted growth, bronchial and pulmonary conditions, poor eyesight, industrial accidents – all these were commonplace, despite an increasing volume of legislation and philanthropic anguish.

When, by late century, compulsory schooling made possible a more or less national assessment of children's physical condition, the outcome – predictably – was appalling. Working-class children were smaller, lighter and far more unhealthy than their social superiors. It is true that, as the century advanced, the working class were taller and heavier than their parents and grandparents. Set alongside their superiors, however, they resembled a lesser breed. They had rotten teeth; in 1892 of 1,000 board schoolchildren in London only 137 had 'sound dentition'. Their eyesight was almost as bad; in some late century schools, normal vision was an exceptional phenomenon. A very high proportion of children in late Victorian Britain had defective hearing. Although middle and upper class children suffered their own (and by modern standards dreadful) levels of physical infirmity, this was never on the scale of their plebeian contemporaries. Not surprisingly late Victorian medical and social investigators became increasingly alarmed and vociferous abut the physical state of the nation's young. To the gloomiest of minds, especially those obsessed with the dire prediction of the eugenics movement, the physical disabilities of British children spelt disaster for the nation; the future was bound to be one of declining fortunes as enfeebled children became inadequate parents and bequeathed their physical (and mental) inadequacies to their offspring.

More positive souls saw a way out of this downward spiral: compulsory medical examinations at school, appropriate (and free) medical treatment, balanced school meals where appropriate, further limitations on child labour, and further protection of the child at every turn. It was true of course that many, if not most, of these maladies traced their roots to benighted domestic circumstances. But it seemed obvious to many that the state could, and should, off-set the worst of inherited or environmental deprivations by the provision of suitable medical and nutritional care. These provisions were initiated in the early twentieth century, but the problems they tackled (however feebly at first) were clear and unavoidable by the time of Victoria's death. The accumulation of evidence began to edge people towards the idea of the state as a tool of social improvement.

Babies and children were only the most obvious of groups harshly afflicted by contemporary patterns of death and illness. When in 1842 Edwin Chadwick reported on the sanitary conditions of the labouring people, he remarked that 'the deaths caused during one year in England and Wales by epidemic, endemic, and contagious diseases' amounted to 56,461; 'the effect is as if the whole county of Westmorland ... or the whole county of Huntingdonshire, or any other equivalent district, were entirely depopulated annually ...' Whooping cough alone killed 10,000 each year at mid-century – and was much more virulent in towns than in the countryside. Similarly scarlet fever struck most severely in towns; between 1859 and 1875 it was the cause of 4–6 per cent of all deaths in England and Wales. Epidemics of typhus accounted for thousands of deaths: 19,000 in 1837, 17,000 ten years later. Typhoid, a disease closely related to dirt, made similar devastating attacks on the population.

But if any one ailment afflicted the British, especially the urban poor, worse than others, it was TB. Like many other ailments, the disease had begun to decline towards the end of the century (by which time social and urban improvements had begun to make their impact on patterns of disease). Nonetheless TB killed one Briton in six throughout the nineteenth century, taking a greater toll each year than all the other major infections put together. In 1838 alone 59,000 people died from the disease in England and Wales. Indeed the contemporary concern with pulmonary complaints was one of the powerful reasons behind the recommendations of doctors and others to quit the pollution of the towns for visits to the countryside and seaside. The awareness that towns were dangerous created the British urge to flee to the fresh air.

There are, of course, major problems with the evidence about illness. Diagnosis and recording was often faulty, and the labelling of ailments sometimes differed from present-day practice. There was, too, enormous disagreement about the precise causes of this or that illness or disease. But time and again, investigations (often of a statistical rather than a medical nature) pointed to the foul conditions of the urban environment – whether of the home, neighbourhood or workplace – as the proximate cause of a host of ailments that blighted the Victorians. How to control and to improve that environment became as pressing an issue as the scientific and medical problems raised by the ailments themselves. It is not to minimise the efforts of generations of scientists and doctors (themselves professionalised in these years) to argue that the beginnings of an effective campaign against national illness came from the social and political drive to clean up the towns.

The problems of the towns were dramatically highlighted by the ravages of the cholera epidemics of 1832 and 1849. The first wave killed more than 30,000 people as it spread across the country from Sunderland. There was no defence against it and local (and national) authorities panicked or were overwhelmed by the scale of the distress. Arguments raged among doctors, the older school attached to the 'miasma' theory of contagion, holding that the infection passed through the air.

It was not until 1854, after elaborate research in Soho, that Dr John Snow conclusively revealed how best to tackle the disease. His conclusions were simple but important. To put an end to the disease he recommended the introduction of

good and perfect drainage
an ample supply of water free from contamination with the contents
of sewers, cesspools and housedrains
habits of personal and domestic cleanliness among the people
everywhere.

Even though the evidence was clear enough, the implementation of the necessary legislation and the establishment of effective bureaucracy was to be the source of recurring political arguments, particularly between Westminster and the localities, throughout the second half of the century. Moreover a thorough-going cleansing of British cities would involve a complex, expensive and far-reaching process which would reach inevitably into every physical nook and cranny of individual and collective life.

Faced by these monumental difficulties, medicine revolutionised itself in Victorian Britain. The first and most crucial step was the analysis of medical statistics, pioneered by William Farr from

1838. Farr and his team were able to pin-point medical problems by careful analysis of the statistics of illness and death. Professional organisations were founded to regulate and control medical education and research. Specialist literature such as the *Lancet* (founded 1823) was published, and legislation enabled teaching and research to be put on a modern, more scientific basis. Similar developments took place in nursing and pharmacy, with the result that, by mid-century, British medicine had taken on its modern form. One major consequence of the professionalisation of medicine was to create effective monopolies; only recognised medical bodies were authorised to sanction the varied practices of medicine, surgery and treatment.

Hospitals, initially, were dangerous places. In 1859 Florence Nightingale wrote, in her book *Notes on Nursing*:

> It may seem a strange principle to enunciate as the very first requirement in a Hospital that it should do the sick no harm. It is quite necessary, nevertheless, to lay down such a principle . . .

Her example was slow in gaining ground in Britain. There were only fifteen nurses a year trained at St Thomas's by the Nightingale Fund in the 1860s and still only twenty by the 1880s. But they went on to become the basis for the reformed nursing staff of the late century. Modern hospitals themselves emerged from the workhouse hospitals and represented a move away from the old voluntary system towards a state-funded system of medical provision. For much of this period it was rudimentary. But the outline of the system we use today can be seen in embryo.

As the medical profession came under greater control the dislike or distrust of doctors, so common a feature of plebeian history in the 1820s and 1830s, gradually gave way to tolerance and acceptance. Even in the tense years of the 1830s and 1840s there were many examples of valiant doctors working for little reward in appalling conditions among the urban poor. In fact most of the evidence brought forth from the poorest urban quarters came from the efforts of such doctors, often employed by the poor law guardians for a nominal fee to deal with their local poor. This was one of the few occasions when the poor had regular access to formal help. For much of the century, the great bulk of Victorians relied, in times of illness, not upon doctors or hospitals, but upon the practice of traditional folk medicines and upon local, communal expertise.

There was in many respects no clear dividing line between

'THE APPEARANCE AFTER DEATH OF A VICTIM TO THE INDIAN CHOLERA WHO DIED AT SUNDERLAND': C. 1832

NIT-INSPECTION IN SCHOOL

SEEBOHM ROWNTREE

GENERAL WILLIAM BOOTH

EDWIN CHADWICK

formal and folk medicine – certainly not before the mid-century. Traditional medicine, folk medicine, was dominant, with its host of rituals inherited since time out of mind, to stave off illness or to restore good health. The use of animals, significant potions or important words, elaborate ceremonies which looked, to the modern mind, like mere witchcraft; all these and more formed a medical system which passed from the 'traditional' world into modern, urban industrial life. Local or travelling quacks, herbalists, and most important of all, local women well versed in coping with the trials and tribulations of life, were more important than formal doctors for much of the population until late into Victoria's reign. Even then, scientific medicine was never able to dislodge the folk traditions, especially herbalism, from common practice and belief. This was particularly true in the important area of pregnancy, childbirth and childcare where the wisdom (sometimes the foolishness) of experienced women in the community provided medical care. Even though drugs were controlled after 1868 (before then opium was freely available in local corner shops), herbalism provided as basic a medical code as the new drugs issuing from formal pharmacies. Often, the new large drug companies incorporated the old substances into new products and made their fortunes in winning over the British public. There were, it is true, harmless, and sometimes dangerous, concoctions flooding on to the market, but the major companies – Beechams and Jesse Boot for example – began their rise to their modern fame by successfully administering to the ailments of the British urban people. Jesse Boot expanded into proprietary medicines in 1874; by 1900 his company owned 181 branches, and by 1914 560. The nation's consumption of patent medicines was extraordinary; half a million pounds' worth was bought in 1850 and four million pounds' worth by 1900. The reliance upon such medicines was an indication not only of the general inadequacy of existing medical facilities but, more importantly, of the degree to which minor but widespread ailments continued to afflict working-class life. But it was also an illustration of the commercial potential available, even among the poor whose pennies could, with the right idea and inventive marketing, be tapped and converted to a commercial advantage.

In the last years of Victoria's reign it was perfectly clear that the health of millions of Britons was poor; a source not only of widespread pain and discomfort to the sufferers but also a matter of continuing concern to social observers of all political persuasions. The evidence from the nation's schools, from recruitment data and from contemporary drug purchases all confirmed the reports readily available from medical sources – notably the district medical officers – that the British were unhealthy in many crucial respects. Indeed there was a convergence of evidence from very different quarters and sources, all of it serving to illustrate a central and depressing fact: the world's greatest industrial and imperial power was seriously weakened in its domestic urban heartlands. For those who thought of the future in military terms (or even in terms of sport) the element of ill-health and of national physical inadequacy was a cause of deep concern.

A great deal of effort had already, if ineffectively, been invested in tackling the nation's ailments. There had been, from the early 1830s, no shortage of advice or evidence about how to tackle the problem. As early as 1832 J. P. Kay (later Sir James Kay-Shuttleworth) had graphically illustrated the link between the filth of industrial Manchester and the physical problems of local working people: 'When the health is depressed by the concurrence of these causes, contagious diseases spread with a fatal malignancy among the population subject to their influence.'

It was the statistical studies of Sir Edwin Chadwick, notably his *Sanitary Report* of 1842, which cut through much of the earlier moralising about the nation's ailments. His report illustrated the different mortality rates between social classes and between different districts of the same town (a system of analysis very similar to that adopted about sixty years later by Rowntree in York). More important, the report – a monument to statistical analysis – established the indisputable connection between disease and the environment. How else could one explain the fact that death rates were twice as high in one part of a city as in another?

More than that, Chadwick 'turned current social theory on its head' by showing that crime, vice, drunkenness and so on 'were the results of the domestic physical environment, not the other way round'. This may seem a simple and fairly obvious point to many modern readers, but it was a major departure for early Victorians and had important ramifications for social policy. To believe that poverty and disease were functions of personal failings was to argue that little could be done about them. To locate their causes (largely if not completely) in the environment was to claim that they could be improved by changing that environment. This was to be a fundamental plank of social reform thereafter (although the debt to Chadwick was often overlooked). In time indeed it was to become an article of faith that merely to improve social conditions would in itself improve personal behaviour. Experience in the western world since 1945 has suggested, however, that the relationship is much more complicated and that human failings cannot always be amended by enlightened social policy.

Chadwick's report was a best seller, a remarkable fact for a report about sanitation, but while it is true that he helped to prick the contemporary conscience, he faced an uphill struggle to implement his ideas. He was first and foremost a difficult man with many, and growing numbers of, enemies intent on thwarting his work for reasons of their own. Moreover his ideas for sanitary reform demanded a complete and costly re-appraisal of medical and engineering practices. Doctors and engineers clashed repeatedly about how best to improve the urban habitat; local politicians were generally reluctant to spend the necessary money:

> There was no glory to be gained in washing sewers with cold water, laurels were only to be won by the builders of Town Halls.

Towns were now entitled to levy rates for such improvements – but to tax the inhabitants was invariably an unpopular move, even for municipal improvement. Thus this apparently straightforward and laudable ideal fell victim, in town after town, to in-fighting between the conflicting groups competing for political power. Not for the last time, the indisputable interests of the people were subordinated to questions of political power in the towns. On top of that struggle there emerged a distinct but crucial clash between the localities and Westminster. Local politicians jealously guarded their own bailiwick and fiercely resisted Westminster's attempt to impose solutions (in this case, sanitary reform) from London. Even the 1848 Public Health Act, the culmination of these arguments, was limited in its power because its central officers were hampered by powers conceded to the local authorities. But by mid-century a start had been made in establishing centralised scrutiny of the health of urban Britain. The clash was henceforth one between centralisation and local government about improving the urban environment, and thus the health of the majority of the British people. In the words of an article in *Fraser's Magazine* in 1847, 'We look upon local government, then – at least for sanitary purposes ... as a popular delusion, condemned by common sense and everyday experience.' Despite vociferous objections from those who disliked interventionism, it appeared to many that central regulations or supervision provided a better guarantee of improvement than the traditional local *ad hoc* system.

Improvements in public health were more commonly wrought through local Acts of Parliament, granting local authorities the powers to clean up their communities. But the drive to ensure that the process continued, and that public health in the towns was not abandoned to the parsimony of local politicians, came, from the late 1850s, from Sir John Simon. His work culminated in the Sanitary Act of 1866, an Act which, though later amended, established 'the vital principal of uniform and universal provision of sanitary protection, with compulsory powers of enforcement in local authorities'. The resulting organisation was to develop from these mid-Victorian origins into the mid-twentieth century Ministry of Health. Simon, unlike Chadwick, was able to get his way, and supervised later laws which tightened up the process of cleansing British towns. Inevitably, political in-fighting characterised the debate and implementation of new Acts. But the Public Health Act of 1875, introduced by Disraeli, was to remain the basis for control over public health until the 1970s.

The system remained a mosaic, a federation of local initiatives and centralised control, with undoubted weaknesses. Nevertheless, by the last quarter of the century there was in place a legislative and administrative system of public health the prime purpose of which was to ensure the health of urban Britain. In the process a rudimentary bureaucracy, forerunner of the modern state, had come into being, employing professional civil servants wielding power over large numbers of people. This trend to centralisation, the intrusion of central government into the lives of ever more people, was a source of political dispute, though politicians of varying persuasions came to be convinced of its necessity. Late Victorian life saw the rehearsal of the argument which was to become more strident in Edwardian life: that collectivism – state intervention – offered perhaps the only way of coping with Britain's urban problems. The Conservative politician, Stafford Northcote, argued in 1869 that

in some respects the intervention of the government is much more necessary now than it used to be in former times; and . . . social questions are assuming such large dimensions that they cannot be adequately dealt with except by the employment of central administrative machinery . . .

His argument was that 'the imposition of Government is often needed' in order 'to prevent the weak and the helpless being made its victims, and to secure fair play to individuals'.

There were, it is true, fierce and articulate opponents of this drift towards a modern, collective state, but the process and its proponents grew in size and numbers. Moreover, their arguments seemed both persuasive and no less relevant by the late century. By every criterion, there was a marked improvement in the nation's health, notably from the 1870s to 1900. These were the years when many of the improvements in the urban environment began to show their effects. The overall mortality rate fell from 23 per thousand in 1855 to 18 per thousand in 1895. Sanitary and urban improvements were obvious, in the form of better urban and personal hygiene, better food and higher wages, cleaner domestic and safer working environments. It is true that in these same years, professional doctors began to administer to ever more people, taking over the traditional role of the priest. But the consequences of their work are much less clear. Historians of medicine are now convinced that few of the major improvements in the well-being of the British people can be attributed directly to formal medicine. This is not to deny the importance of many areas of medical advances, nursing and surgery, but the key source of improvement remains the remarkable changes brought about in the nature of British towns and cities.

For all that unquestioned improvement, the British remained an unhealthy people. If at Victoria's death her subjects were more prosperous and healthier than at her accession, contemporary levels of poverty and related illnesses continued to distress observers. Of course moral and cultural values had changed; attitudes towards human suffering were clearly more refined, more sensitive, in 1901 than in 1837. Allied to this was a stronger belief in man's ability to control his fate and environment, and a rejection of that fatalism characteristic of earlier generations. Few in 1901 could seriously argue, as one might for example in 1801, that nothing could be done about human pain and suffering. It was manifestly obvious that, in the west at least, mankind had begun to exert a dramatic influence and control over his own individual and collective well-being. But it was equally clear that the major improvements had emerged by collective endeavour; by the introduction of a network of political and administrative bodies supervising the well-being of the urban populace.

4

THE FABRIC OF
URBAN LIFE

BY 1901 almost 80 per cent of Britons lived in towns and cities.
There they developed their own sense of place and identity. That
identity was largely shaped by the major institutions they belonged
to: the home, workplace, local community, place of worship, and
later the school. Much of this fabric of Victorian urban life survives
today. But how much of it was new – or different – to Victorians
themselves? Throughout Victoria's reign British towns continued
to grow and to change. At her death, certain towns were expanding
more rapidly than ever: Cardiff, Glasgow and Belfast especially. In
most towns the new 'suburbs', a term introduced in the 1890s, were
growing on the rural fringes of the towns. Some of the British, and
especially the English, were opting for less crowded suburban
homes. The very great bulk of the population, however, had little
choice in this matter and continued to be born into and reared in
the most abject of homes. Domestic overcrowding was the norm for
many British people. One-half the population of Scotland and
one-sixth that of London lived in overcrowded homes with more
than two people per room. The flight to the suburbs, by those with
money, was perfectly understandable. They left behind towns and
cities the state of whose physical fabric was the basic cause of many
of the people's problems. Nowhere was this more obvious than in
the home.

It may well be true that, for most working people, the actual
types of housing were no worse than those of their rural ancestors
or contemporaries. But it was the concentration of poor conditions
which made life so much worse for the generality of people. The
pace of growth of British cities, especially in the first half of the
nineteenth century, created that web of social problems which
proved so troublesome throughout our period. Where to house
these armies of town dwellers? When existing space – in attics,

cellars and the like – was filled, speculative ('jerry') buildings sprang up.

The nature of housing varied enormously between the towns, depending on geography, local traditions and materials. Leeds perfected the 'back-to-back'; Glasgow was characterised by its large tenement blocks. Many were unquestionably badly built, but demolition of some in the twentieth century has also revealed how substantial they often were. They also proved more durable than many of their modern replacements. What made the new working-class housing of Victorian Britain bad was its general lack of amenities: row after row, street after street, thrown together with little or no access to water or sewerage systems, no lighting, no paving and little access to light.

Where local companies existed to provide these services they were, inevitably, overwhelmed by the scale of the problems. The local authorities, such as they were in the earlier years, were powerless against this tide of humanity. Structures of government which derived from medieval villages (in the case of Manchester), and legal powers which were themselves ill-designed to improve the fabric of modern development, all served to compound a sense of helplessness. Moreover, when improvements did take place, they tended initially to be in the better-off areas, for those whose rates paid for the improvements.

Of course it is impossible to disentangle domestic conditions from the broader environmental setting. In the thirty years before Victoria's accession there was a gradual accumulation of evidence from local doctors, pointing to the harmful habitat in which growing numbers of the people lived. But it was Edwin Chadwick's *Report on the Sanitary Condition of the Labouring Population of Great Britain* (1842) which published the first array of statistics.

The importance of better housing was widely accepted. A character in Disraeli's novel *Lothair* (1870) remarked: 'If the working classes were properly lodged, at the present rate of wages, they would be richer. They would be healthier and happier at the same cost.' Large numbers of houses were built by private contractors each year, reaching peaks in the late 1870s and again in 1900 but rarely on a scale or at a price to satisfy plebeian demand. Victorian housing has been considered a success by some historians, but it still left many homeless and many more enduring abject conditions. Most homes were built for renting, which devoured insubstantial working class wages. The very poor simply rented a room or a shared room; overcrowding characterised domestic life for large numbers of working people. Describing the city's notorious slums in 1832 a Liverpool businessman wrote:

In all the houses we visited, with a few exceptions . . . each single room from eight to eleven feet square . . . is inhabited by one, sometimes two, families, in which they both eat, drink, cook, wash and sleep.
    These houses are in general in a dilapidated state, with broken doors, mouldering walls tumbling to ruin, broken windows, in some cases no windows at all, and some without fireplaces . . .

Time and again, a new street rapidly descended into slum conditions as rooms were quickly filled by more people than buildings were designed for. When middle class families moved out to better homes in the suburbs, the poor moved in. The problems were made worse by demolition and re-building, notably by the building of railway lines, stations and marshalling yards within the cities. London was worst hit by this; perhaps 120,000 people lost their homes to make way for the new stations.

Proximity to the place of work was the key factor in choosing a home. In the new industrial towns, housing development had to be within walking distance of work. The late-century development of trams and trains enabled some to live further away in cheaper suburbs and to use the working men's special trains or fares. But for the great bulk of the working population, being close to work was vital.

At the end of our period only eight out of twenty-eight London boroughs were able to record any improvement in their attack on slum clearance and overcrowding. In 1902 C.F.G. Masterman wrote in *From the Abyss*:

Place a disused sentry-box upon any piece of waste ground in South or East London and in a few hours it will be occupied by a man and his wife and family, inundated by applications from would-be lodgers.

There was, as in other areas of social policy, a progressive diminution in overcrowding. But as late as 1891, figures showed that 11.2 per cent of the working population were living in overcrowded conditions; this had decreased to 7.8 per cent in 1911. Yet in parts of the capital the figure was more than one third of the population, with strong variations from district to district. Then, as now, and not surprisingly, rents in London were far higher than in other towns. It was the accumulating evidence about London housing and homelessness which persuaded some people that the unrestrained free market in housing was playing havoc with the lives of millions.

This was a theme to which a number of important novelists returned for their inspiration. In the works of George Gissing the 'urban world was barren, barbaric, beyond amelioration'; a world whose image was penetrated by Charles Booth's researchers after 1889. What they discovered was no less horrible, but much less fanciful, than the world of the novelists. The scale of the problem of urban wretchedness was fully revealed by Booth; he also suggested certain solutions. To modern readers some of his ideas – removal to penal colonies for instance – may seem extremely harsh. But migration, whether forced or free, was a recurring theme among other commentators, from General Booth of the Salvation Army to Cecil Rhodes with his vision of the colonies as an escape route for the overcrowded British poor. For many late-century politicians, the expanses of the newly conquered or settled colonies offered a seductive solution to an overcrowded Britain. Africa, Canada, Australia, South America seemed to beckon as a solution to many British social problems. By the last twenty years of Victoria's reign, the empire and colonies had become prominent in political life, not merely in the arguments about Britain's economic and international greatness, but as an integral aspect of the drive to improve the urban heartland of Britain.

There were, however, other more prosaic solutions. Charles Booth became convinced that better wages, together with pensions for the old, would help to ameliorate the squalor of the labouring poor, a suggestion later endorsed by Rowntree in York. In London, where the problem of housing in certain areas had actually worsened in the thirty years to 1890, the need for municipal housing and vigorous slum clearance required a degree of national or municipal intervention in the free market, which was anathema to many contemporary politicians. Yet Booth and others were convinced that only major and comprehensive state intervention could tackle the full range of urban problems. In their view, people would eventually improve themselves, if only the state or municipality would provide some encouraging assistance.

In general Victorians were reluctant to contemplate spending money on home building or improvements for the poor. An Act of 1851 had permitted local authorities to build homes for working people but by the early 1880s only three towns – Liverpool,

Huddersfield and Nottingham – had availed themselves of the Act. Other Acts of the 1860s and 1870s widened the power of authority to renovate or demolish. Sometimes when such Acts were used, they simply added to the problem by decreasing the housing stock. Determined efforts were made to ease the problems by the development of charitable housing schemes, such as the Peabody Trust, and by Octavia Hill's scheme of closely supervised room rentals, but these and similar initiatives barely nibbled at the problem. In Birmingham, Joseph Chamberlain showed how a vigorous municipal drive with private builders could make major inroads in local slums. Even then, his efforts and his results were limited. Yet he was right to argue that it was folly 'to talk about the moral and intellectual elevation of the masses when conditions of life are such as to render elevation impossible!'

Although there were undoubted developments in late Victorian council-built housing for low income groups, it is by their public buildings – few more spectacular than the town halls – that the Victorian city fathers are likely to be remembered. An Act of 1890 encouraged municipal housing schemes: by 1904 more than eighty towns had borrowed about £4¼ million to that end. But the enormous cost invariably intimidated local authorities. However clear the evidence for patchy improvement in housing conditions by the end of our period, the revelations about the ill-health of urban Britain continued to create alarms about the consequences of poor housing. There were, then, various factors sitting uncomfortably together. The data about the physical weaknesses of urban Britain was widespread and indisputable; but pleas for the state to intervene in the crucial area of housing were rebuffed by the continued insistence on voluntaryism. Legislation enabled, but did not oblige, politicians to act against the worst scourges of poor housing. In the words of one recent historian commenting on housing, 'The State exhorted, but refused to insist'.

Not until the twentieth century was the state drawn more fully into the housing of large sectors of the British people, in large part as a result of the ravages of warfare and the need and opportunity for creating a better national habitat. Yet even by the first years of the twentieth century the evidence, accumulated over previous decades, pointed in the direction of state involvement. There was, however, nothing inevitable about this. Matters could have continued much as they had throughout the second half of the nineteenth century, but that would have involved a tolerance of domestic conditions which stored up dangers for the future. The

BIRMINGHAM CITY HALL

'HOCKTIDE' AT HUNGERFORD: CONSTABLE AND TUTTI MEN

physical ailments of Victorian – and Edwardian – Britons were manifestly a result of their urban environment. Great improvements had been made in that environment by the turn of the century. But home for millions continued to be not that scene of domestic bliss so commonly portrayed by the proponents of bourgeois domesticity. Rather it was a place of overcrowding, ill-health, high mortality and damp and ill-lit discomfort, as depicted in Robert Roberts' brilliant commentary, *Classic Slum*.

Henry Price, a self-taught cabinetmaker, penned his own gloomy verdict on the contrast between the image and the reality of hearth and home:

> The Merry Homes of England Around the fires by night. Someone had sung about them. But they could not have known much about them. The vast majority of them in Towns and Cities have no rooms to be merry in.

That invaluable guide to plebeian life in Victorian Britain, the working-class autobiographer, often told a similar tale about the home. It was not, generally, 'seen as a refuge but as a cockpit, the arena in which the consequences of exploitation and inequality were experienced and battled with'.

Housing was only the most obvious feature of Victorian towns and cities. Victorian people were, as the century advanced, served by an increasingly complex web of services for their needs and, later, for their pleasures. Water, gas and lighting, transport and paved roads, new institutions (hospitals and shops), places of recreation (public houses, music halls, parks and stadiums) – all served, together, to change the face of late Victorian towns. In the establishment of these various facilities, contemporaries argued about their costs and about their broader social virtues, not all of which had obvious economic benefits.

Most worrying of all Victorian urban problems was what to do with the dead. There was no room for more bodies in city churchyards. Gradually, order and decency were imposed. Between 1852 and 1899 Parliament passed forty-five Acts regulating the problems of burial. Some of the new cemeteries were commercial but most were municipal. New landscaped cemeteries were developed on the fringes of the towns. By the early twentieth century the cemeteries, like the parks, had become a venue for visits and walks. A Blackpool newspaper in 1908 reported that 4,000 people visited the local cemetery each Sunday in summer. This was a far cry from the horrible scenes of the early nineteenth century and provides further evidence of the overall improvement in the fabric of urban life.

Perhaps the most durable of popular images of Victorian life are those of the workplace and especially the factory. For the first half of the nineteenth century the factories were small and restricted to certain industries. At mid-century only 411 of 1,670 employers in textile spinning employed a workforce larger than 100. In engineering four out of five employers had fewer than ten workmen. Not until the late century did the scale of operations expand in the major industries such as textiles, engineering and the like. Throughout, legislation and intervention became a feature of the new industrial enterprises, though it was often ineffective to control the worst excesses of long hours, dangerous conditions and poor pay. Much of this legislative protection arose, initially, from Tory philanthropists. By mid-century, notwithstanding its failings, it had been accepted as part of the state's obligation to its people. In the words of the *Westminster Review*, 'legislation to control industry expressly on behalf of humanity and public morals, marks a new era in our social life.'

Nevertheless, in 1900 there were armies of people who remained unprotected by industrial legislation either because of ineffective laws, or because they worked in occupations for which it was notoriously difficult to legislate. This was true for instance of domestics, agricultural workers, and women and children in sweat-shops and workshops. Throughout the period the place of work was the cause and the setting of a host of illnesses and infirmities. The people at work were often already debilitated by domestic conditions, or working in their early and susceptible years. Large numbers of them of course also worked in the open air, exposed to the elements and generally unable to keep warm or dry, to change into fresh clothing, or to eat or drink properly to sustain them through their exertions.

Protection was sometimes provided by legislation, but it was generally resisted by vested interests who imagined their economic concerns were at odds with their employees' well-being. There were, it is true, enlightened employers, Robert Owen for example, and co-operative ventures by labour and management, to secure better working conditions. But it was legislation – state interference – which was most notable in mitigating the worst excesses and dangers of working conditions in a number of occupations. Economic change often created new groups in need of new protections. This was especially true in the sweated trades of the late century.

Only the state and its agencies, however embryonic they might seem in retrospect, seemed capable of tackling the interrelated problems affecting the country's ever-increasing population. Most material improvements which came the way of the British people were a function of private enterprise and initiative, and this was as true of the early as of the late century. The goods and services, the clothes and foodstuffs, the commercial pleasures and delights were the creation of a myriad of industrialists, entrepreneurs and financiers transforming the economic and social base of the nation. But there were limits to what private enterprise could achieve. This was particularly striking in the provision of urban amenities.

Gas, for example, became increasingly important for lighting, but the early private companies (like the water companies) often found themselves incapable of making adequate provision. Gas, like water, was often the cause of bitter local political arguments, as the municipal interventionists struggled with the supporters of private enterprise for control over local supplies. Profits from local gas were sometimes viewed as an alternative to rates for municipal developments. When, from the 1880s, electricity services were developed, municipalities, from the first, involved themselves in its installation, and by the turn of the century two-thirds of the electrical facilities were controlled by local authorities. In the case of local transport services, city trams and later buses, developed as a hybrid system. Often they were privately developed, but gradually the local authorities took over a growing number of them. By 1905, 161 of the nation's 276 local transport systems were managed by local authorities.

At the time of Victoria's accession, the Church of England had been slow to respond to the growth and shift in population. But as the century advanced, places of worship, like the chimneys of home and workplace, began to dot the urban skyline. Nonconformity grew rapidly, particularly in the newer industrial communities. Methodism was at its strongest where Anglicanism was weakest. In Liverpool, Glasgow, Manchester and London, Irish immigration led to a major revival of popular Catholicism. In response the Church of England began to take its gospel to the urban people.

It was never completely successful in this drive; surveys continued to point to the decline in church attendance. The Church of England and its religious rivals nevertheless built thousands of new churches. Whereas only twenty-eight new Anglican churches were built in the decade 1801–10, 401 were built between 1841–45, and 427 between 1866–70. Some of those churches remain among the architectural gems of mid and late Victorian Britain. They were rarely used to the extent their planners hoped, certainly not by the lower orders. In 1845 Engels reported: 'All the writers of the bourgeoisie are unanimous on this point, that the workers are not religious, and do not attend church.' The 1851 religious census showed that of a population of 17,927,609 only 7,261,032 attended church on the day of the census. Such a percentage today would be greeted as a sign of devotion; Victorians viewed it as evidence of religious decline.

In the 1851 religious census, in Booth's surveys and in a host of local studies, it was clear that while the middle classes went to church in droves, working people were reluctant worshippers. In Booth's words, 'the great masses of the people remain apart from all forms of religious communion'. Late Victorian churches and chapels were not, with regional and class variations, as full as we might imagine in retrospect. Cleanliness, like godliness, was a middle-class badge, used to distance the worshipper from his inferiors.

Another building familiar to us today but new to the late Victorians was the large city-centre shop. Although the daily and weekly shopping habits of working people tended to be satisfied by local, corner-shop facilities, the development of relatively large city-centre retail facilities began to change shopping habits and the appearance of the Victorian high street both in city centres and the suburbs from the 1880s. Many of today's major food stores, clothing and shoe shops, chemists and restaurants first established themselves in late Victorian cities. In more plebeian communities, their place was taken by the local Co-op. By World War I more than 20 per cent of all retailing passed through these new shops and stores. The typical shop, however, remained the small corner shop; the major shop was often too distant, too remote from working-class communities, especially in hard times when travel costs seemed high.

The late Victorian town was more varied in its facilities and functions than most British towns had ever been, with the exception of the capital and possibly the old spa towns. It contained a number of major new institutions which, if rooted in older forms, had by 1900 firmly established themselves in the Victorian landscape. The workhouse, asylum, prison, barracks, hospitals, police stations, board schools and, of course, the town halls, of Victorian Britain can often still be seen in British cities. The workhouses were built initially under the Poor Law Amendment Act of 1834. Many have subsequently been absorbed by present-day health authorities, normally as hospitals or mental hospitals. The local poor law authorities were also responsible, by the turn of the century, for the expansion of hospitals in urban areas.

Police stations, which were built close to the troublesome parts of town, usually the poorer, working-class districts, were another reminder of major change in late Victorian life. Where once the British had been renowned as an ungovernable people, late Victorians were famous, with the occasional flurry to the contrary, as a peaceable nation. The police station and its occupants were often unpopular in plebeian communities. The middle classes saw them as guardians of their propertied security; working people felt the proximity of the station and the police patrols in their streets as an intrusive presence, not obviously in their own interest but designed to safeguard the well-being of their betters. Throughout these years, attacks and assaults on police were regular occurrences, especially at times of local or national tension.

Prisons, which are dealt with in Chapter 6, were, like the town halls, extraordinary monuments, not simply of Victorian architecture but to contemporary penal policy. They are also monuments to the manifold social and personal difficulties of governing and controlling so urban and complex a society as late Victorian Britain. How to punish their criminals perplexed the Victorians. It seemed inevitable that a growing population spawned an ever-larger prison population. The Home Office exercised close scrutiny over the nation's jails and new custom-built prisons were constructed in most of the major cities. Pentonville was a model; separate confinement ensured no contamination by other prisoners. By mid-century more than fifty new prisons had been constructed on the Pentonville system. However harsh we might now find the discipline and the regime, the standard of living in those prisons was far better than many inmates might expect outside them. The conditions were, moreover, much less dreadful in many respects than exist in those same overcrowded cells today. In the last twenty years of Victoria's reign, the prison population fell quite markedly. Whereas it stood at 28,700 in 1880, by 1900 it was 17,500 (though it rose again to 22,000 in 1910). In 1983 it was 51,000.

In all these institutions, including the post-1880 elementary schools, discipline was, by modern standards, severe. Often it involved corporal punishment, but punishment was not its only means. It was dictated by the clock and by the machine; hours were

QUEEN VICTORIA'S GOLDEN JUBILEE PROCESSION RETURNING FROM
WESTMINSTER ABBEY, 1887

parcelled out to useful ends, to inculcate industry, application and, of course, to make possible the working of the institution itself. Not all Victorians went to prison, to hospital or clashed with the police, but, after 1880, more or less all went to school. Late Victorians became accustomed, in a way their forebears could scarcely have imagined, to spending part of their lives in an institutional environment, most commonly the school. This exposure was to develop to an even more pronounced degree in the twentieth century, especially with the spread of modern hospitalisation.

The end result was that Victorians became gradually accustomed to working in large buildings and to institutional experiences in a way we might think normal but which was, in fact, quite a recent idea. It became widely accepted that many of society's pressing needs and its problems of crime, health, education and training could only be handled adequately through large-scale institutions. In all of these institutional solutions to late Victorian problems, the state took a hand.

In the process of changing and modernising the fabric of urban life, whether in road building and street paving, sanitation or transportation, education or health, there emerged inevitably new forms of social organisation, new bodies centrally or locally constituted, charged with overseeing the new schemes. By Victoria's death a complex structure of civil administration existed, sanctioned by law and controlled by professionals. By 1901 there were 116,000 civil servants, most of whose work was devoted to superintending areas of the nation's well-being previously left in private hands.

Many politicians and philosophers viewed the interventionist state with alarm. Early socialists, understandably, approved of it. Other critics tolerated it as an improvement on the worst excesses of unrestrained capitalism. In the words of the economist Alfred Marshall:

> the nation has grown in wealth, in health, in education and in morality; and we are no longer compelled to subordinate almost every other consideration to the need of increasing the total produce of industry.

To its most strident proponents, this late-century interventionist state was the tool to end deprivation; 'to remove the excessive inequalities in the social condition of the people' (Joseph Chamberlain). But such views were also to be found among Conservatives.

The expanding state had its determined opponents of course. The *Economist*, in 1895, was blunt:

> However it is looked at economically, State interference in the dominion of civil life and with the machinery of production is an evil.

It is obvious that by modern standards, the state in 1901 was skeletal, whether judged by cost, numbers of administrators or by its degree of penetration into everyday life. But the state had been limited in its success, especially in enhancing national well-being. The endemic problems, particularly of town life, were a reminder of what was still left to do. The question remained: who was able to safeguard those in need of assistance – the old, the sick, the mad, the poor, the ill-paid, that veritable army of needy, measured in their millions, for whom so few crumbs of material comfort had fallen from Britain's prosperous table?

There is no doubt that Britain was more prosperous. More people were well-to-do, and more were plutocratic. Luxury abounded, in the home, in hotels, theatres, restaurants and in various leisure pursuits. In the words of C.F.G. Masterman:

> We fling away in ugly white hotels, in uninspired dramatic entertainments, and in elaborate banquets of which everyone is weary, the price of many poor men's yearly income . . .

Contemporaries began to talk about 'conspicuous consumption'; but it all seemed, to many, to weigh oppressively on the backs of the nation's poor.

5

CLEAN WATER

The contractor [of the 1851 Great Exhibition] is bound to supply, gratis, pure water in glasses to all visitors demanding it; but the Committee must have forgotten that whoever can produce in London a glass of water fit to drink will contribute the rarest and most universally useful article in the whole exhibition.

Punch, 1851

THE key to most important improvements in British town life was water. And the drive to clean up the water supplies was itself a function of increasing governmental intervention in everyday affairs. When in 1842 Edwin Chadwick studied the water supplies in the nation's fifty largest towns his conclusions were a fierce condemnation of private enterprise. In only six cases were arrangements thought to be good; thirty-one were deemed 'so deficient as to be pronounced bad'. The subsequent legislation of 1847–8 allowed local authorities to take over existing, inadequate water works, or to build new ones of their own. By 1879 413 out of 944 urban authorities supplied their own water; 290 were still supplied by private companies, but it was as late as the 1890s before the supply of domestic fresh water became practically universal. By 1914 two-thirds of the population received their water via public authorities at a capital cost of £53 million – the largest single cost to municipal finances.

This was a remarkable contrast to the early years of the Queen's reign. In most towns then, big or small, supplies of fresh pure water were unobtainable. It became apparent, initially by statistical analysis, that the association between foul water and periodic or endemic diseases was very close indeed. Given the unplanned and often rapid development of British towns, it was scarcely surprising that the vices and dangers of the pre-industrial world were transplanted or incorporated into the towns of Victorian Britain. There were attempts, normally by local bodies, often linked to local government, to provide basic utilities for towns. Such attempts were not only ineffectual but were simply overwhelmed by the scale of the problems in urban life.

In common with most urban dangers, London had long been familiar with the problem of water supply. From the Middle Ages there had been schemes for providing Londoners with piped water either from the Thames or from rivers and springs in the surrounding countryside. Urban growth, however, simply covered over or dried up many of the local water holes, wells and ponds; and the local water table changed as the city spread outwards. These supplies of water were in fact often polluted by the deposit of sewage. Naturally enough, the problem worsened as the population grew. Writing to his wife in 1849, Charles Kingsley said of Bermondsey,

> . . . oh God! What I saw! people having no water to drink – hundreds
> of them – but the water of the common sewer which stagnates full of
> . . . dead fish, cats and dogs, under their windows.

At Victoria's accession the city was supplied by nine different companies, all of whom rationed their supplies to those houses plugged into their systems: two to three hours per day, three times a week was the normal pattern. For the rest, water was to be had at local pumps, fountains, springs, becks, streams or rivers – all of which became ever more polluted and dangerous. Human excrement, refuse from the slaughter-houses and knackers' yards, filth from the tanneries and workshops – all found their way into the Thames, from which an estimated 82 million gallons of water were taken daily. The smell was dreadful, but this had been traditionally true of towns. One Irishman said of Leeds in 1840 that 'the smell was bad enough to raise the roof of his skull'.

Nowhere could rival London for its smells, especially each summer when the 'summer stinks' arrived. Various Acts in the 1840s and 1850s were aimed at creating suitable authorities to purge the capital of its endemic water problems, but inevitably the various authorities either lacked power, or fell victim to political infighting. By the late 1850s little progress had been made, but all was suddenly made possible by 'The Great Stink' of 1858. The House of Commons was particularly troubled by the smell from the Thames: 'the pestilential stench which comes every evening into every window on the river front of the Houses of Commons'

(*Hansard*, 30 July 1857). Matters came to a head on 30 June 1858 when a parliamentary officer noted

> the Chancellor of the Exchequer [Disraeli], who, with a mass of papers in one hand and with his pocket handkerchief clutched in the other, and applied closely to his nose, with body half bent, hastened in dismay from the pestilential odour, followed closely by Sir James Graham, who seemed to be attacked by a sudden fit of expectoration; Mr Gladstone also paid particular attention to his nose.

Two weeks later, Disraeli introduced a government Bill to clean up the Thames, which he described as 'a Stygian pool reeking with ineffable and intolerable horrors'. The Metropolitan Board of Works was authorised to raise rates to pay for the cost of building a new drainage system – eleven years after the first London authority created for that purpose, which had been stymied by political fights. Parliament had been grossly offended by the 'Great Stink' and within less than a month, the necessary legislation was approved. Even more remarkable than this display of instant political resolve was the consequent engineering achievement.

The engineer who designed and built the London sewers was Joseph Bazalgette. His achievement was astounding but, unlike many other Victorian engineering marvels – the buildings, bridges, railways and ships – his work remains invisible and generally unrecognised. His scheme took the sewers east and west, intercepting old systems, using gravity and newly-devised pumping systems, and discharging into reservoirs at Barking for the north side of London and at Crossness in the Erith Marshes for the south. Although sewage still ended up in the Thames, it did so twenty six miles downstream of Tower Bridge. In all, Bazalgette's system involved eighty-two miles of sewers laid out beneath the capital, all constructed of special bricks. When completed in 1865, at a cost of £4 million, the system could deal with 420 million gallons of sewage and rainwater daily. The health of the capital greatly improved, and most of the system is still in use in the later twentieth century.

London was of course only the worst – because the biggest – of such problems. The development of the newer towns, especially the industrial ones, multiplied such problems across the face of Britain. Popular ideas of the early Victorian city often consist of images of a foul, polluted environment lacking even the most basic of sanitary amenities. To a large degree this image reflects the reality. Victorian cities were, as Asa Briggs has shown, greatly different one from another; but in the years up to the 1860s, and in some cases even later, they shared the common characteristic of being foul and smelly. There were, inevitably, variations to this general rule, and, of course, enormous variations within a town. This last fact was of course the basic cause of the extraordinary variations in health and mortality figures between different districts and streets, as Chadwick and Rowntree confirmed. Nonetheless, the foulness of the urban area was a commonplace, to a degree and with a host of consequences which modern western observers might find hard to grasp (unless they were to visit a poor city in the Third World).

In Leeds in 1839, 231 out of the town's 586 streets were 'bad' or 'very bad', mainly because of the mounds of rubbish, ash and excrement heaped in them. In Sunderland, a new town, a local doctor described the 'narrow passages, crowded with the thickly populated houses of the poor, badly paved, with a gutter in the centre, where all the filth of human habitations is needlessly thrown'. Merthyr Tydfil, another new industrial town, was described in 1844 as 'in a sad state of neglect . . . Some parts of the town are complete networks of filth.' It is also true that similar conditions existed in rural communities; but the density of population and the unavoidable concentration of sewage and refuse made city life so much worse than rural life. This was, again, reflected in the differences in the statistics of health and death.

Even at the seaside, which was promoted as healthy and healthgiving, the problems of sewage and water were major ones. There, local political power often rested in the hands of men not keen to promote the resort's commercial attractions. When, in the 1870s, the water supplies of 107 seaside towns were investigated, some disturbing evidence came to light. At Filey, the local water when heated gave off 'an offensive smell, which gave a strong suspicion of urine'. In Clacton, water from a hotel well was 'full of particles of suspended matter . . . decomposing muscular fibre and hairs'. At Margate and Weston-super-Mare, the local water was contaminated by salt and vegetable matter. Many major resorts continued to depend on cesspools, and not sewers, into the 1880s. There were, it is true, major investments by many resorts in the costly urban renewal attendant on water and sewer systems and other municipal improvements, but the problems remained. The Prince of Wales caught typhoid at Scarborough in 1871. Brighton did not divert its sewage from discharging on to local beaches until 1874 – when it flushed them out at Rottingdean. Torquay's beaches continued to be polluted by sewage until 1878. In Ilfracombe, the foreshore was badly polluted until 1904. At many resorts though, the sea remained the obvious place to dump whatever sewage accumulated at local urban sites. At the very towns which Victorians turned to in ever-increasing numbers for their summer holidays or day trips – towns which actively promoted themselves as healthy and enjoyable – the prime urban dangers of sewage and poor water were inescapable. The problem survives to this day.

The inland towns and cities were, however, more troublesome and dangerous. The worst were certain industrial towns where the pollution of concentrated humanity was compounded by the atmospheric and discharge pollution from local industries (not to mention the nuisance created by local industrial noise). Clean water was an expensive commodity which, even when available, was well beyond the pockets of working people for much of the century. People had to pay for their fresh water, if rain water or pump water was unavailable. Water-carts regularly toured the streets selling water by the bucketful.

Those unable to buy often stole. A Dr Southwood Smith of London thought it 'fortunate that air is more accessible than water and that its supply does not depend on landlords and water companies'. In Birmingham local magistrates told Joseph Chamberlain how much they disliked convicting water-stealers 'for stealing that which is one of the first necessities of life. They might almost as well be convicted of stealing air.' In Edinburgh, where water had been in plentiful supply before 1818, the supply began to dry up when taken over by a private company in that year. Thereafter the supply was gradually restricted to those able to pay – and even they found themselves severely rationed. There was in effect an annual summer drought, and this situation continued until 1860. In Glasgow when water from Loch Katrine was piped in after 1857, it cost 5s. to acquire the key to use one of the public taps. And similar stories could be told throughout Britain; wherever new supplies were initiated, the cost of connection normally placed the water far beyond the means of labouring people, even if they were geographically close to supplies. When, as was commonly the case, water became a commercial commodity, serviced and provided by companies seeking profit, it was inevitable that those most in need of it – the poorest, most densely crowded urban communities – were excluded by cost. Furthermore, even when municipal bodies did introduce schemes designed to provide city-wide water for the whole community, political arguments often delayed matters. Ratepayers and their political spokesmen objected to paying for facilities which would benefit those who had paid little or nothing towards the scheme.

Such objections had complex roots, which were firmly located in the changing patterns of mid-Victorian politics. It is impossible to divorce the arguments about water and sanitation from the broader debate about municipal and social improvements. There was a natural, instinctive reluctance on the part of the propertied to part with their money, normally via rates, for schemes which seemed of marginal personal benefit. It was to become a feature of late Victorian and Edwardian political argument, notably through the voices of early radical, socialist and labour organisations, that improved facilities ought to apply universally and be sponsored by the state or municipality. These arguments, which are the precursors of those in the twentieth century, were based on the indisputable inequality of social facilities by the late nineteenth century. Whichever aspect of life we care to examine, the middle and upper classes were well served, the working classes ill served, by the late Victorian years. This was as true in the simple matter of water supply as it was of education. By the later years of the century, propertied life was much cleaner than ever before. And thanks to the scented soaps by then available, 'Respectable people now not only dressed differently from the labouring classes, but must have smelt different.'

Among those inclined to godliness it was a simple matter to place next to it their personal cleanliness. It was an ideal way of differentiating themselves from their inferiors, who tended to be both dirty and godless. John Wesley immortalised the idea that cleanliness was next to godliness but it took a full century for his ideal to become the stuff of British social distinctions. Like so many British social patterns, the cult of cleanliness passed down the social scale, and this is not surprising, given the history of the provision of fresh water in the nineteenth century. Early in the nineteenth century the British remained relatively insensitive to smells and to cleanliness. The Duke of Wellington's daily bath, an idea imported from India, was most unusual. Slowly the habit took hold among the upper classes, but it remained rare until mid-century. Hands and face were washed regularly, but rarely the whole body. By the 1860s, the wealthy bathed daily but the middle classes tended to bathe weekly. Not until baths were provided in newer middle-class homes late in the century did the habit become universal among the middle class.

But how could poorer people, millions of whom even lacked

FARADAY GIVING HIS CARD TO FATHER THAMES;

And we hope the Dirty Fellow will consult the learned Professor.

PUNCH, JULY 1855

METROPOLITAN MAIN
DRAINAGE WORKS:
BUILDING NEW SEWERS,
BOW, 1859

"WATER! WATER! EVERYWHERE;
AND NOT A DROP TO DRINK."

PUNCH, 1849

access to fresh water, do the same? The 'great unwashed' remained unwashed, and would do so until the availability of water changed this age-old pattern. The virtues of personal and collective hygiene came high on the list when all the nation's young began to appear in the elementary schools in the 1880s. There was also a mounting charitable drive to persuade the poor to wash regularly. But to what avail was a speech or a tract, encouraging regular washing, if there was no soap or water? More practical measures did indeed help, notably the philanthropic and later the municipal wash and bath house, though the costs of these tended to be too high for working people once again.

Bleak as this image of the life of the poor may seem, it would be wrong to minimise the remarkable improvements in water supplies by the end of Victoria's reign – a fact more than amply illustrated by health figures. These reveal that medical problems tended to be worst where conditions of personal cleanliness, and access to fresh water, were poorest. Thanks to new engineering systems, fresh water was now pumped great distances into most British cities. Water was taken from Wales to Birmingham, from the Lake District to Manchester; Leicester drew water from the Derwent Valley sixty miles away. Such supplies were not, of course, without their own local political arguments. Moreover the demand for water grew much faster than the rise in population. Manchester's water consumption increased eight-fold between 1850 and 1880, while its population only doubled. The explanation for this fact (and similar evidence is available in most major towns and cities) is of course the changing nature of industry and the rising standards of living. Individuals were using more water; and urban facilities consumed water on a massive scale, through bath houses, factories, swimming pools and homes. By 1876, for example, 80 per cent of homes in Manchester had their own taps; and flushing lavatories, whose use was spreading, consumed growing volumes of water.

But we need to remind ourselves of the limits to this progress. In 1898 Birmingham still had 30,000 pan privies and middens in back yards. In Nottingham, as late as 1901, human waste was removed by steel pails. And even as late as 1909, Gravesend was wholly dependent upon cesspools and well water. Moreover, there were numbers of towns where, though flushing lavatories had been installed in newer homes, the water supplies essential to them remained unconnected. Technical faults, poor installations and neglect, and the continuing poor, irregular or weak supplies of water meant that large numbers of lavatories simply did not work effectively. So, improvements there were in abundance, but there remained imperfections, flaws and gaps in the provision of decent water and sewerage. By the late years of the century urban Britain was still in need of a major clean-up. The 'Big Stink' of the mid-century may have been a thing of memory, but there remained much to be done in the proper application of water.

Two Acts in 1875 pushed forward the cleaning up of the towns. The Public Health Act obliged authorities to instal drainage and sewerage, whilst the Artisans and Labourers Dwellings Improvement Acts allowed slum clearance and permitted authorities to build their own homes (strengthened by subsequent Acts this statute formed the basis for the development of modern council housing). Under the Public Health Act, local Medical Officers of Health were given the necessary support staff and found their own position strengthened. Now no longer subject to the blatant political pressures of earlier years, they were able to tackle their city's problems more vigorously. Public 'nuisances' were removed from the streets by the ton, and a more aggressive approach was taken towards adulterated or rotten foods, one of the century's prime health hazards. By the 1890s doctors were informing their local authorities of the specific geographic areas – the streets, houses or tenements – where sanitation and overcrowding were prime causes of ill-health. Nevertheless, throughout that decade there were a number of outbreaks of disease, notably in Cambridge, Lowestoft and Middlesbrough, which illustrated the continuing hazards besetting certain towns or particular areas within them.

The necessary improvements were still costly; the demolition of slums, provision of water and sewerage continued to offend purse-proud local politicians, often more anxious not to alienate their voters than to ameliorate the lives of the local poor, who were, in any case, mainly powerless politically. But in town after town, or ward after ward, sanitary and housing improvements were followed by marked improvements in the health statistics presented by the medical officers. The process was often slow, and sometimes took a lifetime, but by the turn of the century, these efforts – often spear-headed by a dedicated local medical team – had their reward in the area's greatly improved standard of health. By the early years of this century, it has been argued, the worst examples of overcrowding, poor water supplies and sewerage were to be found not in urban but in rural communities, which were much less capable of raising the necessary capital for improvements.

Above all else it was the availability of fresh water which made the British a healthier people, a change that was not effectively noticeable until the last years of Victoria's reign. As fresh water became more available, attitudes towards personal hygiene and the importance of sanitation began to change. Working people came to welcome officers from the sanitary authorities. It had become clear to all but the most resistant of local politicians that clean water and good sanitation made economic sense. The dire effects of filth, in terms of illness and death, had been a crippling economic burden throughout the century. Among individual members of the poor and the working class the economic burden of caring for their sick relatives and of burying their premature dead had long been a cost they could ill afford. As long ago as 1842 Edwin Chadwick had been at pains to stress the economic cost, to individuals, to families and to the state, of permitting the prevailing levels of urban filth to continue unchecked. It took fifty years for the ideas of that remarkable man to be absorbed into everyday political and social thought.

Britain, quite simply, could not afford to tolerate the old habits of urban dirtiness. Not, that is, if it wished to have a people capable of competing in an increasingly fierce international economy. The main thrust for a cleaner Britain did not come solely from an economic impulse. There was in addition a powerful and growing body of opinion which was deeply offended by the worst sufferings of the poor. Nor was this feeling predominant in any one political party. Men and women of all political persuasions, from within the main Tory and Liberal parties and from the ranks of new, fledgling or fringe political groups, were loud in their criticism of social conditions in British towns and cities. Their outrage was periodically fuelled as now, by the findings of the most recent social survey or publication, or by the local evidence of medical officers. By the end of the reign there had been a quite dramatic change in attitudes towards social conditions, whatever its source. The arguments about how best to solve or improve those conditions continued to rage, and do so down to the present; but by 1901 there was a wide consensus that the nation could not afford, either economically or morally, to tolerate those blights on the urban landscape which had partly characterised Victorian Britain. There was a growing body of opinion by Victoria's death willing to argue that Britain's collective weaknesses were to be measured by – or were a function of – her persistent urban and human problems.

In the campaigns to tackle those problems and to clean up

British towns the work had been undertaken by a remarkably varied army of conscripts and volunteers. To call it a 'sanitary' movement is to make it sound more cohesive but less impressive than it was in reality. Also missing from its ranks were the great bulk of those it aimed to help: the poor people of urban Britain, who were locked into inescapable and wretched circumstances. By the 1890s, they had come to recognise the benefits of improved conditions, but for much of the century their own voices, or those of their rare spokesmen, were generally unheard and certainly unheeded. They were, however, the victims of an urban society which inflicted a terrible price, in individual and collective suffering, upon people unable to help themselves, notwithstanding the importance of plebeian and union politics in these years.

In the course of the century, the state and municipal authorities had effectively begun to cleanse, regulate and make life safe in urban Britain. The worst excesses and blights of urban Britain were made possible by the purest forms of *laissez-faire*. In house building, factory location and in the provision (or non-provision) of urban amenities, the free market of the first half of the nineteenth century took little account of what we might now think of as social or personal costs. There was a remarkable rush towards urban and, later, industrial development, and insofar as it had any single or predominant ideal it was that of profitable expansion. There were, it is true, efforts by some such as Robert Owen at New Lanark and Sir Titus Salt at Saltaire, to establish ideal communities; but these were of little broader significance. They may have shown that other models of industrial or urban development were possible, and that they were economically viable too, but they made little impression on other industrialists and urban developers, whose economic ambitions were rarely checked by the humane need to create a decent or civilised environment. It is no caricature to depict the sum of urban and industrial growth by, say, the 1860s as an apparently paradoxical phenomenon: a janus-faced society, where economic power and urban wretchedness were unsurpassed. The struggle for sanitary reform, to instal fresh water, was, in large part, the struggle to make good the shortcomings of an expansive, and economically buoyant, fledgling urban and industrial power.

To that end, the Victorian state – weak, ill-developed and thinly stretched by modern standards – was brought into being to safeguard the well-being of the British people. Parliamentary scrutiny, legislation, centralised bureaucracies, all interlocked with the development of local, municipal government and administration to intrude themselves ever more closely into the nation's social and economic affairs. It would be wrong to claim that this was on anything like the scale of the 1980s. Nor was it necessarily at the expense of private interests. Although it is clear that the need to control the worst excesses of private ownership and investments lay behind much of the state or municipal involvement by the 1890s, there was no significant call to bridle private enterprise itself (save from those minority socialist groups whose voices were, as yet, scarcely audible). If there was a theory at work here, it was the need to effect a partnership between those with money to invest and the municipal and state authorities whose task it was to monitor the human consequences of certain forms of private enterprise. The provision of water, so basic to all urban ameliora-tion, provides a classic illustration of this pattern. By 1897, 346 of the 960 water authorities were private. The remaining 614 were run by the local authorities themselves.

It was here that we can see in operation that 'Gas and Water' socialism which became the creed of a number of major city politicians who remained at the same time firmly wedded to the broader virtues and benefits of capitalism. Personified by Joseph Chamberlain, the successful Birmingham businessman turned so-cial reformer and politician, this commitment to municipal 'social-ism' became a notable feature of late-century urban politics. Chamberlain made great play with the shortcomings of the local water works company, founded in 1826, as a source of many of Birmingham's social ills, especially among the poor. His theory was simple enough.

> All regulated monopolies, sustained by the State, in the interests of the inhabitants generally, should be controlled by the representa-tives of the people, and not left in the hands of private speculators.

Whilst he did not object to gas works making profits, he felt that 'the Water Works should never be a source of profit, as all profit should go in the reduction of the price of water'. In advancing this ideal which underpinned his argument Chamberlain and others helped to change Liberal philosophy. The old Whig ideal of limiting the function of the state mainly to the preservation of life and property was rapidly relegated to the museum of political redundancies. In its stead there emerged a new political ideal, rooted in the Liberal party, that the state should be the agent for the physical (and, if possible, moral) improvement of the people. This view never enjoyed majority Liberal support, but it prompted a comparable radical response among the Tories, notably Randolph Churchill. The end result was that, by the late 1880s, groups within both major parties, now having to appeal to the newly-enfranchised male working class, had established a beach-head in urban plebeian communities, with the plea for social improvement. Thus, at both local and now national levels, political arguments about contemporary social issues had established themselves in the urban heartlands of Britain.

All this may seem distant from the sanitary condition of Britain and from the main concern of this chapter, water, but this is far from being the case. Political and social arguments about what seems to be a simple matter, such as the provision of fresh water (which in any case was far from being simple) often broadened into a general theory of government and politics. Britain had become a healthier, safer, economically stronger society thanks to those improvements which resulted from fresh water. As we have seen, there remained major urban social problems; but whatever progress had been made had been achieved in large part by intervention and close regulation. To offer a visitor a glass of water by 1901 was not the poisonous gesture it had been a mere fifty years earlier.

6

LAW AND ORDER

LONDON had traditionally posed major problems of law and order. Its massive population, its varied and often inaccessible communities with their own codes and customs and, of course, its persistent levels of poverty, all created a city which was difficult to control. Furthermore the policing systems until 1829 were archaic: ancient bodies, inadequately staffed or trained and quite unsuited to the needs of a major city. Outbursts of urban disturbances – the Gordon Riots of 1780 for instance – were sharp illustrations of the fragility of social control in the nation's major city. In truth, London, and to an even later date most other growing towns, was not policed at all. At night special constables, thief-catchers and private agencies stood guard over urban property and safety. But by day most Londoners, and Mancunians until later, largely looked after themselves. In a society of small-scale communities, such a system was reasonable enough; but the proliferation of towns and cities, and the birth of an entirely different kind of society, meant that policing and the legal control of the people simply had to be rethought and recast.

From the late eighteenth century, this had become the main concern of the authorities in London and provincial cities. The perennial nightmare was of a major urban explosion; the Gordon Riots cast a shadow over city government for years to come. This was at its most acute at times of national political or economic crisis. In the 1790s, in the tense post-war years 1815–19, and in the years of Chartism in the 1830s and 1840s, the gathering of large crowds in towns was a worry. In the main, authorities were concerned about the crowds which gathered for radical or reforming purposes, but also about any large crowds, whether convening by order or spontaneously. The collective cry for the vote was as worrying as that demanding food, or even those voices raised while watching a major popular spectacle. For this reason many traditional forms of popular culture were feared where once they had been tolerated. The massive crowds gathering at a public execution, a parish football match, a London fair, a Lancastrian wakes or a boxing match, all posed serious difficulties for the inadequate forces of law and order.

Such gatherings were, however, infrequent events in the calendar of law-and-order problems. More worrying still was the daily difficulty of keeping the peace in the face of a rising population, layers of whom were permanently denied the basic material necessities of life. Hungry people inevitably stole food and other necessities; this was the most obvious form of crime committed against the propertied by the propertyless. Politicans, in Westminster and the localities, had to consider how to stop or curtail crimes, and how to punish or cure the wrongdoers: in short how to teach the plebeian nation the error of its criminal ways. Though the problem of crime was not simply a matter of plebeian groups offending the propertied, until the 1890s it tended to be seen in those terms; not until then was serious attention paid to the distinctive genre of middle-class, professional crime (often financial).

The history of crime has in recent years become an area of increasing research among social historians. Their findings, along with the work of social scientists, though still incomplete, have allowed us to reappraise this important element of the recent British past. Contemporary literary sources about Victorian crime, despite their evident concern, provide us with only a partial picture of nineteenth-century social reality. More recently the skeleton of Victorian crime has been exhumed more effectively by historians' sophisticated analyses of crime statistics. Victorians were of course great accumulators of statistical data. Few aspects of contemporary life, beginning with demography, were not quickly reduced to statistical form, and buried in those volumes of governmental and private publications which have since become the historians' treasure-trove. It is in fact the wealth of Victorian statistics which has enabled us to reconstruct in such detail aspects of nineteenth-century life.

From the evidence we can draw certain broad conclusions. There was a slow increase in the crime rate throughout the eighteenth century. Crimes against property rose sharply between 1770 and 1800, reached alarming levels in the post-war years (1815–17), and remained a matter of great alarm until the mid-nineteenth century.

From the 1860s, crimes against property and the person declined gradually, for the rest of the century. Can it be mere accident that in the worst years of industrial and urban growth, up to the mid-century, crime was on the rise, and that, as British life became more 'settled' into its urban-industrial routines, the worst excesses of criminal behaviour began to abate? Victoria came to the throne in the midst of national uncertainties: the after-effects of the new Poor Law and the beginnings of Chartism, the popular radical movement which, between 1838-48, sought universal male suffrage. The governing and propertied orders felt that they were living through times of major crisis, one manifestation of which was a rise in crimes against them and their possessions. Yet the onset of better times (for many, if not for all) from the 1860s did not dispel crime; it merely changed it. Those who harboured hopes that economic improvement would purge the nation of its criminality were disillusioned to find that prosperity could nurture crime almost as well, if not as extensively, as property. The distinctive middle-class financial criminals of the late century came from the ranks of the late-Victorian prosperous in the banks and in business.

Crime was not of course a uniquely urban phenomenon. Rural crimes remained considerable, though often different in nature from those in towns. In some places, levels of crime (notably personal assaults, attacks on officials, and destruction of property) were higher in the country than in the more widely troubled towns. Major agricultural protests paralleled the better-known urban protests. But in rural life, where the old landed interest held sway and where their spokesmen in Parliament (or on the bench) were able to defend that interest, rural crimes were more isolated, more obvious, and perhaps more readily tackled and punished. Indeed some of the more celebrated victims of a rapacious legal system such as 'Captain Swing' or the 'Tolpuddle Martyrs' emerged from rural, nor urban, troubles.

The problems of the towns and cities, though, remained more serious, because many of their areas remained inaccessible – urban growth being beyond the reach, and often beyond the control, of the men traditionally in charge of local government and law and order. The beadles, reeves and sheriffs – offices inherited from earlier centuries – were clearly inadequate in the face of the daunting problems of the nineteenth century. It was clear to many that Britain needed properly constituted, modern police forces. Following the French lead and the model of the Irish police, Sir Robert Peel in 1829–30 established the Metropolitan Police, an ill-paid force of 3,200 men, often denounced as a foreign importation: 'The thing is not – never was – English,' the *Standard* declared on 7 December 1829. The force contained a fair proportion of ex-servicemen: they were fit men under thirty-five, a cross-section of working-class London with a sprinkling of Scots and Irish. It was, initially, a demanding job, with long hours, unpleasant work and low pay leading regularly to indiscipline and resignation. Recruitment was best when times were hard.

The police set out to tackle those London scenes

> of drunkenness, riots, and debauchery of every kind (not infrequently accompanied with acts of daring and desperate outrage and robbery upon the unoffending passenger) and the horrible language which met the ear at every turn. (*The Times*, 14 October 1829)

Soon, according to *The Times*, respectable worshippers could go to church without

> witnessing some disgusting exhibitions, or having their ears offended with blasphemous and filthy expressions.

Peel was a Tory reformer, but unlike others around him he was flexible and pragmatic. His work created a police system, under Home Office control, which could face the new challenges created by an urban and industrial society. Though always criticised, particularly by political radicals, the force gradually impressed itself on the city, and on the pattern of crime, not only in London but also across the country when groups were despatched to restore order. New legislation encouraged the creation of police forces throughout urban and rural Britain and by the late 1840s, although new policing was patchy, it was effective and had proved its worth, even if it was not universally popular. By the 1860s, policing had become more widespread and much more professional. But the question remains: what effect did the new police forces really have on crime?

The definition of crimes is often uncertain. Police statistics of arrests, prosecutions or convictions may vary greatly, according to the policies and pertinacity of a local police force. If an officer is determined to arrest and prosecute drunks, there will, naturally, be a reported increase in local drunkenness. In fact this is what initially happened; drunken and disorderly offences greatly increased in the wake of a new police establishment. This happened, for example, in Manchester in the 1840s. In 1869, the incidence of arrests for vagrancy in Bedfordshire increased threefold; the police had been instructed to be vigorous in prosecuting vagrancy. Despite such difficulties of interpretation, it seems that Victorian crime reached its peak in the 1840s, and historians of crime have seen an undoubted deterrent at work in the form of the local police force. But it was also significant that the local poor were, at the same time, under closer scrutiny (mainly by the poor law authorities) and their involvement in local crime was consequently reduced. There are, of course, immense difficulties in interpreting such evidence, but it seems clear enough that the police were essential in gradually reducing crime.

This is seen most clearly in the area of public order. Large public gatherings, which were so worrisome to the authorities, were pacified, though dangerous outbursts of mass violence did occur late in the century, notably the Hyde Park Riots of 1886. Political meetings and popular cultural gatherings became peaceable where they had once been turbulent or threatening. In Oldham, the local workers' holidays had been known for the rowdy scenes around the local rushcart ceremonies. Fights between rival rushcart gangs finally precipitated action by the new police force.

After 1849 the police and the local fire brigade became basic elements in the curbing of popular, criminal excesses in the second half of the nineteenth century. The police imposed public order on the British urban people to a degree few could have imagined possible. In the early years of the nineteenth century, the British had been infamous as a volatile, ungovernable people. A century later, they had acquired that reputation for collective tranquillity which was not to be shattered until the new urban disturbances of the 1980s. In the streets, and in the alleys and courtyards of Victorian Britain, the police were immensely successful. Policemen tackled those 'problems' of urban life – the drunks, the beggars, the urchins, the prostitutes: that army of social casualties cast adrift on the streets of Victorian cities. In rural life much the same pattern emerged; the police brought to court offences which had rarely been viewed as crimes earlier. There too they completed the rout of popular culture; following directives from the bench they wiped out the surviving excesses of popular custom which had lasted for centuries.

The results of the fight against theft and burglary were less clear; the police's initial successes were limited. They dealt effectively with some of the old criminal ghettoes, but their major successes against indictable crime had to await the improvements in policing, particularly in its technical aspects, in the last twenty years of the century. Whatever their failings and shortcomings, the police were in great demand from those with homes, businesses or properties to protect. These late Victorians looked to the police as the natural protectors of their material lives. But in the early years of their establishment in a number of towns the police incurred a marked degree of plebeian hostility. Violent attacks against policemen were frequent up to 1870, in part because the police had to implement a string of unpopular laws – against vagrancy, the poor, poaching, and against juvenile offenders. Working-class communities felt themselves to be the permanent object of suspicious scrutiny by a vigilant and unsympathetic police force. The location of new police stations and the inescapable foot patrols in poorer communities left no doubt as to which parts of town were deemed to have a policing problem. Gradually, however, a reluctant tolerance of and even support for the police crept into working-class communities. Working people no less than their propertied betters were quick to demand protection from the police. In the words of David Jones, the police

> not only offered everyone the prospect of greater security, but they also became involved in primitive forms of social work.

Crime was one of the issues which earnest Victorians debated throughout the century. Was it a disease, made worse by life in the town? Was it hereditary, bequeathed like family traits from generation to generation? This latter notion was easily dispelled by evidence from Australia, where the descendants of transportees quickly broke the mould of their ancestors' criminality to establish themselves in a range of successful urban and rural occupations.

Why did towns and cities require more policing, i.e. more policemen per head of population, than other communities? London had one policeman per 349 people, other towns one per 672, but the counties managed with one per 1,134. Once more, the focus of concern was the urban community and the poorest sections of its towns. Was alcohol a cause of crime? Both seemed inextricably linked in the urban mire. Did the poor commit crimes because of their wretchedness? In retrospect, the evidence on this point seems clear enough; the gradual decline in indictable offences was most striking when material conditions showed a notable improvement in the late century. Assaults on the police fell sharply in the late 1870s and 1880s, and it seems likely that elementary schooling played a role in limiting the drift of children into organised crime. From the 1860s, when police forces had established themselves as natural features of the British townscape, crime began to show a marked decline. This was also true of years when the economy entered a new phase. There were, too, the zealous efforts of bands of nineteenth-century politicians and businessmen anxious to cleanse their neighbourhoods of the wickedness they saw in a great deal of plebeian behaviour. The urge to impose 'respectable' behaviour on urban and plebeian life was a recurring theme in late-century local politics and policing; to draw the common people away from their less-easily policed habits. The local drunks were isolated and exposed to the rigours of arrest and prosecution. Much the same happened to prostitutes, who were arrested in droves in all major Victorian cities. Research on Victorian prostitution shows what we might logically expect: that it was linked directly to levels of poverty. Gladstone was only the most famous of many Victorians keen to learn more about the lot of those wretched women who haunted the streets and regularly appeared before the courts. They, along with so many other wrongdoers, found themselves caught up, in the late century, by a much more effective machinery of law enforcement and prosecution. Policing and the law had to become progressively more efficient as the century advanced. The state itself had become more powerful and more intrusive, and was able to demand levels of policing, and to expect a degree of adherence to the law, which would have been unthinkable only two generations earlier. To quote the words of a recent historian of crime, 'The balance of power and technical knowledge was clearly on the side of the State.' Indeed, much of the machinery of the embryonic modern state was created in order to pursue the fight against crime. The late Victorians were guaranteed their recently-won social tranquillity largely because of the intrusion of the state. If Britain had become, by Victoria's death, more law-abiding and orderly, as the crime statistics indicate, it was largely the state's doing.

New policies to deal with convicted criminals were part of the continuing Victorian debate about crime. The major reform of British prisons had long preceded Victoria's accession, and found its inspiration in the late eighteenth-century shift in humane sensibilities. Transportation had been a common sentence in the early nineteenth century, but it was the new prisons which characterised early Victorian optimism in the power of isolated incarceration to reform the criminal character. Not everyone agreed with current policies. Dr W.C. Taylor wrote in 1849:

PRESTON: 'ATTACK ON THE MILITARY', 1842

THE CHAPEL, PENTONVILLE PRISON, 1862

PRISONERS AT CLERKENWELL HOUSE OF CORRECTION LONDON, AT THE
TREADWHEEL, 1874

Wandsworth Gaol,

County of *Surrey*

28 Decr 18*72*

PARTICULARS of a Person convicted of a Crime specified in the 20th Section of the Prevention of Crimes Act, 1871.

Name .... *John Hanks 4088.*

and

Aliases ....

<table>
<tr><td rowspan="11">Description when liberated.</td><td>Age (on discharge) ....</td><td>*16*</td><td rowspan="11">
Photograph of Prisoner.</td></tr>
<tr><td>Height...</td><td>*4 ft 11*</td></tr>
<tr><td>Hair..</td><td>*Brown*</td></tr>
<tr><td>Eyes ....</td><td>*Brown*</td></tr>
<tr><td>Complexion....................................</td><td>*Fresh*</td></tr>
<tr><td>Where born....................................</td><td>*Kingston*</td></tr>
<tr><td>Married or single ....</td><td>*Single*</td></tr>
<tr><td>Trade or occupation ....</td><td>*Printer*</td></tr>
<tr><td>Any other distinguishing mark ....</td><td>*Scar*</td></tr>
</table>

left arm, small mole right side of neck, & scar on back

[17198.]   E. & S.—20,000.—9/72.

PRISON PARTICULARS ON A DISCHARGED YOUTH OF 16, WANDSWORTH GAOL, 1872

> We have found that morals are not, like bacon, to be cured by hanging; nor like wine, to be improved by sea voyages; nor like honey, to be preserved in cells . . .

With the decline in transportation, imprisonment became a more popular weapon of penal policy. Pentonville was opened in 1842, and in that decade more than fifty other prisons were opened on Pentonville's solitary-cell principle. Derived from Jeremy Bentham's famous design of a 'Panopticon', prison design concentrated on isolating prisoners, and based itself on the example of current penal policy in the USA. But harsh punishments remained, including the crank, the treadmill, and being deposited in a hole in the ground. Though enlightened when compared with the past, it was a system primitive and often cruel to modern eyes. From 1854, separate reformatories were launched for youthful offenders to isolate them from hardened criminals. Though funds were generally local and often voluntary, all came under the close supervision of the Home Office. An increasingly interventionist state worked closely with voluntary agencies to reform, if not to solve, this major social problem. The prison and reformatory became an integral element in Victorian penal policy, their ideal of isolation designed to prevent the contagion of crime and criminal ideas. The degree of isolation involved was extremely cruel and drove many inmates beyond the limits of endurance and reason. Yet the same can be argued for the chronic overcrowding of these same prisons by the 1980s. The prisons of Victorian Britain, though new, reformed and with their administration inspired by an idealism which today looks ill-placed, were loathed and feared by those who endured them. This did not prevent offenders returning time and again. In Victoria's reign, the prisons of England and Wales registered 15 million receptions; many were on remand, some were for a few days, four out of five were for less than a month. Prison was a familiar experience, however fleeting, for a substantial number of plebeian Victorians.

In the course of Victoria's reign the more brutal aspects of penal policy were gradually mitigated. The eighteenth century had seen an increase in the number of capital offences entered in the statute book. By the beginning of the nineteenth century there were some 200 such offences. Paradoxically, however, as the laws multiplied, the actual executions decreased. There was a sustained campaign to reduce these offences still further, pioneered by Sir Samuel Romilly, and slowly, Parliament whittled down the number of capital crimes. By 1861, the number of capital offences had been reduced to four – a figure unchanged till 1957. Moreover only a minority of those condemned to die were, in the end, executed. Of the 8,483 sentenced to death between 1828–1834 only 355 (less than 5 per cent) were actually killed. We might still feel an average of sixty executions a year a horrible level of life-taking, especially as historians of crime can find few traces of its alleged deterrence. To make the situation even more ghastly, public executions survived until 1868. They attracted vast crowds, often in the tens of thousands, and formed part of that bloody element in popular culture which so many reformers sought to suppress. To make matters worse the new railway companies ran excursion trains to neighbouring executions. Towns were awash with visitors to see the spectacle: country people walked into town, local workers left work early to watch, and adults often took their children along. A 'ringside' seat perched in a neighbouring building could command a high price. Yet for all its attraction, the brutality of the killing and the frequent incompetence with which it was often administered, generally shocked or sickened the crowds. This was the situation a quarter of a century after Victoria's accession; public executions were not finally banned and confined within prisons until 1868. *The Times* reporter at the last public execution (of an Irish Fenian, convicted of firearms offences, and hanged in May 1868) commented:

> Most assuredly the sight of public executions for those who turn to witness them is as disgusting as it must be demoralizing, even to all the hordes of thieves and prostitutes it draws together.

The arguments against public execution were fierce and involved large numbers of prominent Victorians; Dickens was among the most remembered abolitionists. Sometimes the debate strayed over into a general attack on capital punishment itself. By and large, however, abolitionists were content to remove executions from the public view. The vast crowds which were attracted to public executions could not easily be controlled or marshalled. In fact there were regular incidents of violence and sometimes of death in the crush of the execution crowd. It was an archaic survival, in stark contrast to the more refined sensibility of the mid-Victorian age.

Despite periodic alarms about the level of late Victorian crime, it was generally confined to specific areas and communities within certain towns and cities where crime and law enforcement undoubtedly remained troublesome. Parts of east London remained a policing problem throughout the century. It was no accident that such communities had not only higher levels of crime but also endemic economic problems. Crime remained closely tied to poverty, but many of the poor came to public attention not for their poverty, but for breaking various laws. The drunk, the vagrant, the prostitute, the truant represented the poor in the docks of British courts. Of course not all crime stemmed from the poor. Changes in the economy and the spread of material prosperity created many new opportunities for entrepreneurs, both legal and illicit. 'Prosperity-based crime' was striking for its novelty, but it constituted a relatively small phenomenon.

At the turn of the century, when the British had become a highly urbanised people, they appeared to be losing their criminal ways. Britain was much less plagued by serious crime than it had been a century before. Was this because the people were town-dwellers, the inhabitants of a highly successful industrial nation? As the towns had grown, so too had a complex structure of law, to safeguard most aspects of urban life, from water to education, along with sophisticated policing systems. More laws and more policemen seemed to have made the British more law-abiding and peaceable. But actually the disciplining of the people was a function of a myriad of institutions – family, community, workplace, place of worship, school, all encouraging in their own ways and for their own interests an attachment to law-abiding and generally obedient behaviour. Of course it is also true that there was a great deal of self-interest in being law-abiding. The general spread of material betterment from the 1880s provided ever more people lower down the social scale with material items and styles of life they wished to protect. The 'respectable' working class, as much as the middle class, had much to gain from peaceable law-abiding behaviour; they were no less outraged by petty thefts or habitual drunkenness. Thus the late Victorians were peaceable and law-abiding not out of fear of the consequences of transgressing, but from a clear appreciation of the benefits to be gained from keeping within the law.

In large measure the acceptance of law and order was a direct result of living in a highly urbanised world, itself subject to detailed regulation and control. The state had clearly established the major guidelines for individual and collective behaviour to a degree which early Victorians would have found bewildering. But the state, or voluntary agencies, seemed as yet incapable of solving problems which continued to plague urban life. The crimes of the poor, like their poverty, reminded even the most optimistic of late Victorian reformers of how much remained to be done.

7

EDUCATING
THE PEOPLE

DURING Victoria's reign, a major transformation came over the education of the British people. In the early nineteenth century, education for the lower orders was viewed with suspicion; at worst subversive of the social system, at best merely unnecessary. While their betters resisted the education of the poor, the poor themselves generally saw little virtue or advantage in acquiring it. There were, however, remarkable examples to the contrary; of hardworking and sometimes brilliant working men and women who taught themselves. The recent past had been decorated with examples of humble men reaching eminent positions, having been noticed at an early age and given a formal education.

As the nineteenth century progressed two broad factors worked to encourage the spread of popular literacy and learning. Firstly, the maturing economy demanded basic literacy from more and more people, particularly from women in the last quarter of the century. Secondly, those in authority came to fear ignorance in the urban masses, where once they had feared learning.

From 1763 to 1815 there had been a marked connection between popular literacy and radical politics. In the Wilkes movement, the American Revolution and later in the corresponding societies in the 1790s, labouring men and tradesmen had found their literary appetites satisfied by cheap radical publications, from the works of Tom Paine to the outpourings of the provincial and London newspapers. In 1775, for example, 12.6 million copies of newspapers were sold; by 1782 there were fifty newspapers in the provinces. All of this was in addition to an amazing volume of printed ephemera – handbills, squibs, ballads and the like. Not surprisingly it was above all an urban phenomenon: these were the very areas troubled, in those years of great social and political stress, by radical politics.

Governments of all persuasions tried to prevent, and then to control, the spread of popular literacy. In the words of Hazlitt,

> When it was impossible to prevent our reading something, the fear of the progress of knowledge and a *Reading Public* ... made the Church and State anxious to provide us with the sort of food for our stomachs which they thought best.

Governments secretly subsidised friendly newspapers, and harassed their opponents. The Stamp Act – reduced in 1836, repealed in 1855 – was a weapon in the government's armory, for it made newspapers too expensive for working people: it was effectively a tax on newspapers. Yet the attachment to publishing and reading survived and spread, thanks in large part to the unflinching efforts of generations of brave though persecuted writers, editors and publishers. Ironically, both sides were convinced of a central proposition, that 'knowledge is power'; one side sought it, and the other refused to concede it.

It was, however, a battle which the established order was bound to lose. The changing urban order, the development of an *ad hoc* and later a national education system, the technological revolution in printing, papers and inks, transportation and news-gathering, all created an utterly different society, and one in which the printed word was sought by millions. Publishing became a highly lucrative business; books, magazines and newspapers were sold in their millions. Indeed, by the end of our period, British life was characterised and directed by the printed word to a degree no one could have predicted. By 1901, to be illiterate or semi-literate had become a personal disadvantage. The Post Office bears testimony to this fact. When the penny post was introduced in 1840, 132 million letters were delivered in England and Wales. By 1870 this had risen to 704 million; in 1913 it stood at 2,827 million. This was in addition to the 1,069 million postcards delivered in the same year. In the 1890s, there were twelve deliveries a day in the City of London; properly posted and addressed, a letter might arrive within four hours of despatch. Late Victorians kept in touch with each other by the written word to a degree we can now scarcely envisage.

The battle for a free press, which was so bitter an issue at Victoria's accession, had been won, and transformed the press into an extraordinary success story by the late century. From the 1860s, Victorian newspapers flourished; prices fell, circulation grew and titles proliferated in London and the provinces. Thanks to the telegraph and the railways there emerged the phenomenon of the genuinely national newspaper. Through their columns the British readers, now counted in their millions, were better informed, bombarded with political views of many complexions and urged, via seductive advertising, to purchase a vast range of new goods and services. Alongside the local and national dailies, there developed the 'serious' weeklies with sales in excess of most present-day weeklies. At the lower end of the market, there were the local evening papers, with their diet of scandals, and the often sensational Sundays, with circulations as high as half a million by 1870. In the last twenty years of the century the press changed quite dramatically. The 'new journalism', pioneering new techniques of presentation and campaigning, won over millions of newspaper buyers and raised their sales to new levels. The British had by Victoria's death become a nation of newspaper readers. In 1900 the *Daily Mail* sold 1 million copies a day.

Books too were read in abundance. Libraries had become popular in the 1860s, though intially they were private subscription libraries. By the late century (and thanks to an Act of 1850) local authorities began to establish their own lending libraries. By 1918 there were 438 in England, and their number of books grew from 1,800,000 in 1885 to more than 9 million in 1914. The lower middle classes and self-improving working men bought novels by the millions, able to do so thanks to the new cheap editions produced by a number of publishers. Two obvious factors made possible this mass market for the printed word; firstly, a literate population, able and keen to use its reading abilities, and secondly a readership with spare cash to spend on newspapers, novels and the like.

Literacy is so widespread (in the west at least) that it is easy to overlook how new a phenomenon it is. Although it came into being in its modern form, nurtured by formal schooling, in the nineteenth century, Britain had long been notable for its literacy among the common people. In the pre-industrial world, levels of literacy varied enormously. Local studies show that, in general, women were less literate than men. In 1760 in parts of Yorkshire 64 per cent of men but only 39 per cent of women were literate. In London at much the same time 94 per cent of men and 74 per cent of women were literate. In general, literacy was higher in towns than in the country. But it is confusing to speak of national percentages, for these figures break down into a mosaic of local (often parochial) and sexual variations. What seems clear is that, in its early phases, industrialisation had a harmful effect on literacy.

In Ashton-under-Lyme, it fell from 48 to 9 per cent between 1823 and 1843. In the 1860s, at a Manchester sewing school, only 199 out of 963 (21 per cent) girls could read and write. In those towns where the new industries depended heavily on child or young adult labour, the education of the young seems to have been badly retarded.

Yet conditions did get better. By the mid-century between two-thirds and three-quarters of English working people could read. In 1865, 61 per cent of the men in the navy and marines could read well and only 11 per cent not at all. By the late 1870s, those able to sign the marriage register with only a mark, and not a signature, had fallen to 1 in 7 men and 1 in 5 women.

There was, then, wide though variable literacy in Britain long before the coming of compulsory schooling in 1880. Many continued to dislike education for labouring people. The scientist, David Gilbert, had argued in the Commons in 1807:

> However specious in theory the project might be of giving education to the labouring classes of the poor, it would in effect be prejudicial to their morals and happiness: it would teach them to despise their lot in life, instead of making them good servants to agriculture and other laborious employments to which their rank in society had destined them.

Such views were widespread and had arisen not simply from the hostility of the propertied to the threat from the lower orders, but also from the well-tested links between popular literacy and radicalism. There is an abundance of evidence to confirm the widespread support for the views of one farmer's wife, who thought

> the lower orders were fated to be poor and ignorant and wicked; and that as wise as we were, we could not alter what was decreed.

Even an educationalist uttered similar thoughts, remarking on the risks of

> elevating by an indiscriminate education the minds of those doomed to the drudgery of daily labour above their condition and thereby rendering them discontented and unhappy in their lot.

It was clear that there were serious risks in the *status quo*, in allowing ignorance to prevail among those growing armies of people confined in the squalid and restricted spaces of urban and industrial Britain. Some form of learning – limited, religious perhaps, and consciously manipulative – was needed. Suitable schools in towns 'where the rising generation are training up in ignorance, wickedness and forgetfulness of God' would educate people 'in his fear, in knowledge of his ways; and in the daily remembrance of his commandments'. The Church, especially the Church of England, had traditionally been in control of most educational facilities existing up to the late eighteenth century. Despite powerful objections, it became involved in the educational changes of the nineteenth century.

The most important innovation was the establishment of Sunday schools, launched in 1787 by Robert Raikes and Hannah More. Their inspiration was the ignorance of country children, but the schools' main influence was to be in the towns. Hannah More had wanted the schools 'to train the lower classes in habits of industry and piety'. But as the schools increased, they changed – not always to their founder's satisfaction:

> In many schools, I am assured, writing and accounts are taught on Sundays. This is a regular apprenticeship to sin. He who is taught arithmetic on a Sunday as a boy will, when a man, open his shop on a Sunday.

The numbers attending were remarkable: 450,000 in 1818 and 2½ million by mid-century. The methods used to teach, and the syllabus employed, had tremendous limitations; but for millions of Britons, the Sunday school opened the door to literacy and learning, and to a lifetime's attachment to a particular church or creed. Indeed, the Sunday school was responsible for a number of key aspects of plebeian popular culture in the second half of the nineteenth century. It was also to leave its mark on politics and the unions, for many working-class leaders up to 1914 were influenced most by the literature, the lessons and the learning acquired initially in Sunday schools and chapels.

Other schools were opened, on a voluntary and primarily religious basis, to educate the poor. In the years after the French Wars, the Church of England vied with the free churches to establish even more schools; the 'National' schools versus the 'British' schools. This established a rivalry for the minds and the religious attachments of British children which was to continue, in differing forms, into the twentieth century. Government was drawn in for finance and supervision, and by 1850 was providing almost £200,000 towards educational costs. Legislation also obliged factory owners to teach their young apprentices, though this was often ignored or ineffectual. A study of 427 schools attended by factory children in 1857 revealed that only 76 were good, 146 were thought 'inferior', 112 'worse than indifferent' and 66 'positively mischievous'. A similarly bleak picture emerged of education for the very poor, under the terms of the 1834 Poor Law Act. Not until better pay became available for the teachers (after 1846) did the education of pauper children become effective. Even then, the prevailing concern of those educating the poor was in keeping with the overall attitude towards poor law administration: the need to minimise costs, but also to secure compliance and peace among the poor.

Much of the purpose behind these various educational changes was the need to keep the young, and hence future generations, in check. Schools were essential, it was argued, in the new industrial and urban environment, to inculcate those personal and collective virtues among the labouring people which would fit them for their place, their work, their rewards and their roles. Dr Kay-Shuttleworth expressed the point perfectly in 1846:

> Supervised by its trusty teacher, surrounded by its playground wall, the school was to raise a new race of working people – respectful, cheerful, hard-working, loyal, pacific and religious.

But Kay-Shuttleworth was also a great educational pioneer convinced, from his own work on the education of paupers, that the state should supervise education. He was also responsible for laying the basis for the creation of a modern teaching profession.

By mid-century a remarkable change had come over the propertied attitudes towards popular education, helped in part by the efforts of Prince Albert. Where once it was considered dangerous, it was now thought to be essential; 'We need not dread the over-education of the people – the better they are educated, the better men, the better citizens they will become.' But alongside this ideal – of imposing education from above – there existed a powerful independent educational tradition in working-class communities. There was, for example, a host of working men, keen to learn, to improve themselves through mastery of the printed word, and for whom education was not simply a means of consolidating their natural social (or sexual) role in the world. Many sought learning, however rudimentary, for its own sake or as a means of advancement. But we must remember that throughout our period, and for the great bulk of the population, education, if it existed at all, was not a means towards personal or social advancement; it was not a means of rising up an easily-climbed ladder. Education, for most, was designed to consolidate the rank, the sex role, the social position, of those receiving it. There were, it is true, large numbers of influential and wealthy men who, by the early years of the twentieth century had risen, initially through education, from humble positions to ranks of great eminence – in state, business, finance and the church. But such educational mobility for a few provides precious little insight into the prospects or the reality for the many.

Slowly, and largely reluctantly, the state was drawn into education. For the first decades of Victoria's reign voluntaryism held sway, and was fiercely defended by nonconformists anxious to maintain their own schools and influence, and to resist the Anglican-dominated state. The numbers of teachers grew, schools proliferated and the amount of state money allocated to schools rose to £½ million by the late 1850s, though it provided for a mere 13 per cent of the population. The aim of these elementary schools was that their pupils should be able to read newspapers, write a letter or add a bill; most children failed to do so. Payment by results was introduced in 1862 to improve matters ('If it is not cheap it shall be efficient, if it is not efficient, it shall be cheap': *Hansard*). But as the economy improved in the 1850s and 1860s, and as Britain became more democratic after the 1867 Reform Act, broader education became more attractive to employers and more feasible for employees.

The result was the important 1870 Education Act, which established the right of all children to schooling (but did not make it compulsory), and organised it through new School Boards supported by rates and grants. The flaws in that system, and the continuing religious bickering, led to the 1880 Act, which obliged all children between the ages of 5 and 10 to attend school. By 1900, 54 per cent of school children attended their local board school. Teaching by results was gradually replaced, the teaching profession became a highly trained occupation and the syllabus slowly reformed, with an emphasis on 'the development of interest and intelligence and the acquirement of real substantial knowledge'. The '3 Rs' came to be replaced by an education which, for all its failings, had the shape and outline of a recognisably 'modern' system. In 1870 there were some 12,000 'certified' teachers, half of them women. By 1880 this had risen to 31,300 and to 53,000 in 1895 (when three-fifths were women). All had been trained, until the 1890s, by voluntary religious agencies. Thereafter, the new teacher training colleges increasingly took over their training.

What was taught within the new state schools in the last two decades of Victoria's reign was dictated in large part by men who had emerged from the public schools. There was a direct educational link between those privileged institutions and the humblest of inner-city board schools of the turn of the century. Teachers and pupils by 1900 were subject to a system of learning, to a syllabus and to ideals, which were the educational inheritance of a different social world. The public schools had risen to their contemporary fame and influence in the course of the nineteenth century. Initially, they were inadequate and often wretched institutions, but the educational and social reforms, set in train by Dr Arnold and his disciples, revitalised the schools and established a string of new schools throughout Britain. They took in boys from the new industrial and commercial classes, imbuing them with educational and social ideals which derived from the upper reaches of British life. Reared as gentlemen, the late Victorian public school boy might not be ideally suited for the competitive world of late-century business, but he was brilliantly drilled in the manners and virtues of a class whose political power might be on the wane, but whose social style and influence remained undiminished.

In the late years of the century, these schools incorporated the new-found ideals of manliness; of physical, sporting endeavour, of valuing team above self, of learning to play the game and to worry not who won or lost. Sports fields and pavilions became as important as the class room, and in some cases the schools came to value their pupils' athletic prowess more than their scholarly achievements. It was among these young men that most of modern Britain's mass games and sports were perfected and given their modern form; football, cricket, athletics, rugby, rowing – these and others became the athletic diet of the late-century public schools. By 1900, and for related reasons, they had established themselves as the games of the common people, watched by millions and played by tens of thousands.

Public school athleticism spilled from its privileged confines to influence the working-class male world of urban Britain. Through the efforts of school teachers and administrators, churchmen, businessmen and philanthropists, the sporting institutions and ideals were passed on, via Sunday schools, churches, chapels, factories and now, after 1880, through elementary schools, to armies of children. The new athleticism fused with older popular traditions of recreations and popular cultural forms. And it seemed ideally suited to the contemporary obsession with the social and

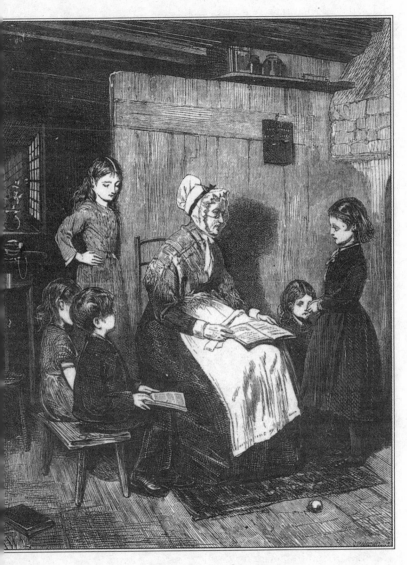

DAME SCHOOL, 1872

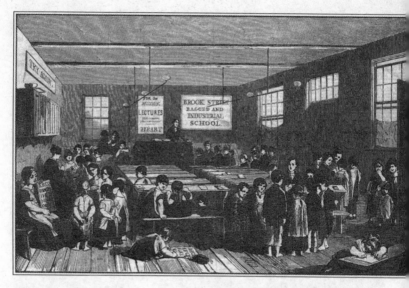

BROOK STREET RAGGED & INDUSTRIAL SCHOOL, 1853

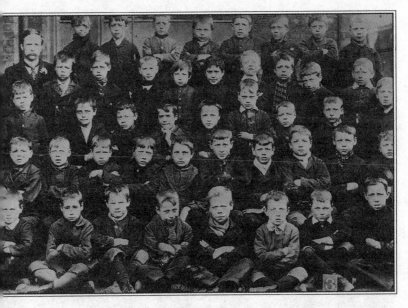

SNOWFIELD SCHOOL GROUP, BERMONDSEY, 1894

THE SUPPER AT SURLEY, ETON COLLEGE, JUNE 4TH 1840

RAGGED SCHOOLS: 'FREE BREAKFASTS FOR HUNGRY CHILDREN'

physical needs of the deprived urban masses. Games and athleticism appeared a perfect antidote to the well-publicised and widespread ailments of the British working class. For those who believed in the mental and physical virtues of athleticism, the encouragement of sporting activity among working-class boys (but not girls) through schools seemed both an ideal end in itself and a valuable blow against one of the nation's basic failings: urban ill-health. Team games, with their strict allocations of positions, roles and functions, had a wider importance for the encouragement of discipline, obedience and collective endeavour.

It would be easy to exaggerate the significance of games. But they clearly had an important social function over and above occupying and tiring the young in school time. Through the schools, the public school ideal was rapidly disseminated into the broad reaches of plebeian urban life. In fact, these sporting ideals quickly spread around the world, taken to the fringes of empire, settlement or trading involvement by public school and working men, their enthusiasm for their new games imitated by many local peoples. Thus, by the end of Victoria's reign, the sports of the public schools had been adopted not only by the British urban masses, but also by a widening international following.

The world of empire also loomed large in the teaching to be found within the new state schools. In lessons, in school texts and notably in geography and history, British children were taught not simply the facts of empire, but urged to glory in it. They learnt to be proud of the homeland, but often in terms that were suffused with ideals of racial superiority. Britain's empire, like her industries and 'civilisation', were described as proof of British superiority. In fact, this sense of superiority was conveyed through children's books long before the late-century apogee of empire.

There were other factors which encouraged a fierce attachment to all things British: popular songs and verses, the music hall, the late nineteenth-century popular press and youth movements. After 1880, when all children attended elementary schools, it is likely that those early school lessons laid the foundations of that patriotism which flared so suddenly and glaringly at moments of imperial crisis – in the Boer War, in other African adventures and in August 1914. There is evidence to suggest that there were pockets of resistance to the prevailing mood of jingoism in the period 1880–1914, but its demonstrations were among the most eye-catching aspects of late Victorian public life.

Why should working people and the poor become so fiercely

jingoistic? What did empire and military glory mean to them, the very group deprived of most of the material benefits of contemporary life? It would be absurd to suggest that they were all duped, their emotions manipulated by politicians and the press. There was evidence of this happening to a degree, but the emotive popularity of imperial issues is more easily explained by the ideals fostered by the schools in pupils' formative years.

The nation had now become highly literate. In schools, as in adult life, much of the literature consumed was dominated by imperial ideals and ethics. Children's texts taught the young about a world in which the British ruled by virtue of their superior race, civilisation and God-given religion. Other peoples, including Europeans, were esteemed, or disliked, depending how closely they matched up to British values and norms. Empire provided authors with colourful stories of British daring, valour and superiority. It was in writing of empire that a number of contemporary writers made their names and fortune, notably G. A. Henty. There were also numerous journals and comics (*Boy's Own, Boys of England, The Young Briton, The Union Jack*), whose tales of imperial derring-do spread the mythical ideals of empire far and wide, up and down the social scale. In schoolroom and in leisure moments, generations of British children were taught to think of Britain as a unique society; freer, more democratic, more blessed than any other and anxious to bestow on its ever-increasing native peoples the blessings of British rule and trade. Rarely were they given a more balanced view, rarely an appreciation of the cruder side of empire: of economic self-interest, the violence and cruelty of conquest, and the importance of indigenous life. Of course, we cannot expect Victorians to behave like late twentieth-century people. But we need to ask ourselves: are the values of that imperial urge so cultivated among the young the ones we might like to emulate today?

There was pride in national achievements and in imperial glory. Much of that pride focussed on the ageing monarch, who in earlier years had been no less unpopular in her cranky isolation. Royal jubilees were the occasion for wonderful pageants of imperial achievement, and the nation marvelled at the spread, the humanity and the artefacts of empire. Schools and learning played an important role in cultivating this attachment to empire. Yet even before the Queen died, it had become clear, in the Boer War, and in the Sudan, that the glories of empire were tempered by domestic and imperial problems. Not everyone living on the imperial fringes approved or welcomed British dominance. At home, many young working men were unfit to join an army whose task it was to dominate the empire's lesser breeds. It was as if there were lesser breeds at home, people who had little to show from the industrial wealth, the imperial expansion or the growth of compulsory schooling in the years 1880–1901. At Victoria's death, her subjects were an educated people. But they were educated to particular ends. Moreover technical and scientific education was already lagging behind that in Germany and the USA. British education had other deficiencies. Not least it lacked, at the elementary level, the encouragement of critical scrutiny. People were educated to fit their social rank and their sex role within that rank. Education was not envisaged as a ladder which people could climb depending on ability. One headmaster wrote in 1889:

Some people seem ever afraid lest the poor be instructed beyond their station.

8

CHARITY AT
HOME

VICTORIANS were generous and unstinting in their work for
charity. There were few worthy causes which failed to attract the
money, organisational skills or energies of Victorians. In fact
among the middle classes charitable work became a way of life,
soaking up surplus energies, especially of their womenfolk, and
salving their stricken consciences. There were, as we have seen,
causes in abundance awaiting their attentions. Charitable activity
became a characteristic feature of propertied life: to be broadcast
aloud, emblazoned in the press, and chiseled onto the side of public
places and monuments. Such publicity guaranteed public sanction
for the do-gooders; it conferred on them the approval of their
peers. Men of wealth displayed their largesse in generous benefac-
tions to the needy, *nouveau riche* businessmen were quick to
publicise their gifts to local charities. It was almost as if the act of
giving money had to be public to be effective.

This was, however, only the public face of a complex story. For
every public gesture, there were thousands of hours of modest but
practical work, as Victorians sought to put right the wrongs of the
world around them. Not all their efforts were directed at obvious
physical human needs. They helped animal welfare (think of the
surviving drinking fountains for horses), they built libraries, large
numbers of which still stand, they staffed the thousands of classes
in local Sunday and ragged schools. There were few aspects of
contemporary social life which failed to lure Victorians to their
charitable stations.

Victorians directed their greatest charitable energies at the local
level. Although there were then, and still are, a number of famous
national charities, much of the activity took place in the local
parish. In London alone in 1885, *The Times* calculated that there
were more than 1,000 local charities with a total income of almost

£4½ million. The range and diversity of their interests can be seen from the representatives at the memorial service in that year for Lord Shaftesbury. Shaftesbury was the very model of Victorian charity; he inspired and attracted to his service not only the obvious and major organisations, but also charities like the Pure Literature Fund, the Cabman's Shelter Fund, the Flower Girls' Mission, and the Metropolitan Drinking Fountain Association. To these and others Victorians gave millions of pounds, often in their wills. A sample of 446 wills bequesting £76 million in the 1890s showed that £20 million of it went to charity. There was no denying the extent of Victorian philanthropy or the energy and idealism behind it. By the mid-Victorian period, however, there were questions as to whether it was properly directed and organised; was it effective; was it securing the returns which all that time and effort ought to have achieved? At times, Victorian philanthropy resembled an army, eager, energetic and vast but at times ill-led, ill-disciplined and often purposeless.

Philanthropy was, then, a broadly-based Victorian phenomenon. But it did not emerge, full-grown, in the late nineteenth century. Charitable works, doing good to one's neighbours, caring for the helpless and the poor, all these had been characteristics of propertied life in Britain for centuries. Contributing towards the care of the poor had long been a feature of respectable social behaviour. Of course, paying towards the upkeep of the local poor had also been resented, but objections were always balanced by an awareness that the money usually bought peace and tranquillity. It was less obvious, however, why a person should contribute towards charity, if it failed to secure social harmony. Long before the accession of Victoria, it had become clear that charity alone could not guarantee social peacefulness.

Social strife had been at its worst in the years of the French wars (1793–1815), when the difficulties of wartime were compounded by those of population growth and economic change. Hunger, poverty and consequent unrest periodically flared despite the efforts of good men and women to bring relief in their neighbourhoods. Similar troubles bedevilled the post-war years, now made more difficult by the early impact of industrialisation. The problem was not confined solely to the towns: the normally peaceable countryside experienced its share of outbursts. These were not simply the result of radical politics, nor would it be correct to suggest that philanthropic efforts on behalf of the poor were inspired principally by the need to head off trouble. How to deal with the poor was, after all, only one concern of a broad philanthropic 'movement' which sought to ease society's basic ills.

Attitudes towards philanthropy changed before and after Victoria's accession. The emergence of a new humanitarianism meant that there were more and more areas which became the proper target of the philanthropic impulse. In the early years of the century, humanitarianism established itself as a major intellectual and social force in British life. Much of it grew from the evangelical movement, but it also derived from a secular attachment to social rights which created a new sensitivity in a broad range of people. The idea that rights belonged to everyone – men and women, young and old, black and white, sane and mad, free and prisoners – entailed better treatment for some neglected groups. Movements, institutions and local groups proliferated to care for and further the interests of all these and others. The mad were now treated in a more humane fashion, prisons were reformed, an array of cruelties (to animals and children) was attacked, slavery was abolished, factory conditions were improved, the inhumanities of military punishments were curbed. Naturally all of these changes involved long and sometimes unsuccessful campaigns in London and in the provinces. By the mid-point in Victoria's reign, the worst abuses apparent in Britain in, say, 1801 had been curbed. By the time of her death, Britain seemed a haven of humanity compared to a century before. This is not merely a 'Whiggish' view of history, a matter of modern eyes viewing history as the gradual but inevitable triumph of progress. There were many examples of Edwardians who looked back with satisfaction on the triumph of humane values in the course of the nineteenth century.

It was not, of course, a universal and consistent achievement. There were obvious areas of neglect and indifference, in fact of inhumanity, even at the turn of the century. Nonetheless, the British had unquestionably smoothed the rougher edges of many forms of their social behaviour. They took great pride in having done so and often felt themselves the superior of other nations, whose record seemed less impressive. Victorians had come to view themselves as a more 'civilised' people, not measured in the formal trappings of high civilisation, but in the humane qualities which slowly came to characterise British social life. Even so, in 1901 few problems seemed more intractable than poverty itself, despite nearly a century of philanthropic effort and seventy years of rudimentary and crude state involvement. It was as central an issue at Victoria's death as it had been at her accession. The Queen came to the throne when the implementation of the 1834 Poor Law Amendment Act was creating controversy across the country. Throughout her reign, periodic revelations displayed the inadequacy of that law, its counterproductive qualities and, most important, the unchanging levels of poverty itself.

Victorian charitable work addressed itself to every kind of poverty, to 'stray children, fallen women and drunken men'. Efforts were often focussed on a specific church, chapel, or a compact parochial area. A soup kitchen, a nightly refuge for homeless children, a ragged school for local children; such organisations absorbed the energies of tens of thousands of Victorians, large numbers of whom were women. To many of them destitution was thought to be caused by moral weakness, and the alleviation of hardship best served by the encouragement of self-help and individual effort. Even so, millions of pounds in charity were poured each year into the bottomless hole of urban poverty: always more each year than the sums provided by the poor law authorities. As fast as the money and the activities were generated and dispensed, new ranks of the poor shuffled forward for food, clothing, shelter and care.

Urban charitable relief was rarely enough to do more than bring temporary or partial succour. Housing trusts barely touched the problem of destitution and homelessness. Ragged schools could never hope to feed, clothe or shelter all the destitute children, and their efforts were limited to a brief period each week. York's Hungate Ragged School was a monument to the selfless activity of bands of young men and women. But its four decades of work took place in an area of York where Rowntree, by 1901, found some of the city's most wretched conditions. It would be callously indifferent to the efforts of those volunteers to dismiss their work as valueless. But who could claim that by 1901 the objects of their concerns were better off?

It is far too easy to speculate on the motives for Victorian philanthropy; to seek origins which might be more psychological than social. For many activists, immersion among the poor undoubtedly brought its inner pleasures. This was especially true for large numbers of middle and upper class women who were denied access to purposeful or organised work. Many turned to the poor, or other charities, as a surrogate career, of which their menfolk approved and to which they gave in abundance. Evangelists urged women to take up the cause of philanthropy. Hannah More, perhaps the most influential female evangelical, wrote:

> It would be a noble employment, and well becoming the tenderness
> of their sex, if ladies were to consider the superintendence of the
> poor as their immediate office and set apart a fixed portion of their
> time as sacred to the poor, whether in relieving, instructing or
> working for them.

There was also the belief that only effective philanthropy would
save the nation from major social upheaval. But a great deal of
charitable work was directed towards foreign causes; to convert or
'civilise' ex-slaves, Indians or other native peoples under British
rule.

Good works marked out a woman or man as a person of standing
in a community. In life, and then in death, charitable work was
listed alongside a Victorian's varied accomplishments and qualities. Who is to say that such work was unworthy (even when
ineffective), or that it was false because it brought satisfaction to
the benefactor as much as to the recipient? Notwithstanding
philanthropy's failings, it is hard to imagine Victorian life without
it. It was a quintessentially Victorian phenomenon. And herein lies
its historical importance.

Charity is important in retrospect as a reflection of those
mountainous social ills against which ranks of Victorian women
sallied forth. The variety, persistence and depth of Victorian
philanthropic activities gives a measure of the social problems of
contemporary life. It was justification enough for any particular
charity to argue that it was tackling one or more of the nation's
major or minor ills. In addition many activists genuinely believed
that they could, through personal example and through the charitable systems they established, reform the objects of their charity;
they could save the dissolute, raise up fallen women, and instil
industry and self-help where it was most needed. They could, they
imagined, help bring about that 'reformation in manners' first
initiated by William Wilberforce, which would by itself purge the
nation of its dissolute ways and destructive social habits.

Many charity workers were especially convinced that their
efforts ought to encourage those virtues of 'self-help' which so
many Victorians took to be the key to the nation's success. To an
extent the concept of self-help emerged as a by-product of the
attachment to individualism fashioned by the classical economists
Adam Smith and Nassau Senior. It was, however, given a more
popular, and much cruder, expression by later writers: Harriet
Martineau, James Wilson in the *Economist*, and finally the well-
known Samuel Smiles, whose best-selling *Self-Help* bequeathed the

TAKING GIFTS TO A
POOR COTTAGER,
1884

SCRIPTURE READER IN A NIGHT REFUGE

BLACKFRIARS SHELTER FOR DESTITUTE AND WORKING MEN
AWAY FROM HOME, LONDON, c. 1903

SALVATION ARMY WOMEN'S HOSTEL

idea to later generations. 'Heaven helps those who help themselves,' intoned the successful Mr Smiles. The deity apparently approved both of personal cleanliness and worldly success. How he must have despaired of the British people, the vast majority of whom were dirty and unsuccessful.

What worried Smiles, and other Victorians, was that philanthropy could be harmful. 'Whatever is done for men or classes to a certain extent takes away the stimulus and necessity of doing for themselves.' What he and others sought was to encourage men 'to elevate and improve themselves by their own free and independent individual action'. With this or similar intentions in mind, many charities sought not only to alleviate distress, but also to teach their wards to manage for themselves; how to budget and economise, how to read and write, how to cook and provide for a family. But for armies of the poor all of these lessons went for naught; no amount of instruction could secure them a roof, a room, or a living wage.

Many mid-Victorians disliked the proliferation of charities, some competing and all of them in danger of rendering their wards dependent and unable to cope on their own. 'One chief cause of poverty [argued the *Westminster Review*] is that too much is done for those who make no proper effort to help themselves.' It was to discipline charities themselves, and to discipline recipients of charity that the Charity Organisation Society was founded in 1869. It was the first serious body to put poor relief on a strictly professional basis based on casework; and it was committed to an unwavering attachment to the ethic of self-help. Led by S. S. Loch, the Charity Organisation Society was, in its leader's words, committed to the idea that 'to be beneficient, charity should assist adequately, i.e. so as to produce self-help in the recipient'.

The Charity Organisation Society went to great pains to discover the personal circumstances of individual destitutes, but it refused to accept that anything other than personal shortcomings could provide an adequate explanation for destitution. Little sympathy or time was wasted on those who refused to accept the stringent conditions for relief. The members of the COS bitterly opposed local schemes of work creation, whether by municipality or whoever else, arguing that they would be artificial exercises which would fail to offer true prospects of self-improvement. Their work received the public support of prominent people, Bishop Temple of London for example, who shared their distrust of indiscriminate and undisciplined alms-giving. Those who dominated the charity movement up to World War I believed that they were engaged not merely in the assuaging of physical need, but in a moral crusade which must be won for the good of the nation. The belief must be inculcated in everyone that they should care for themselves through life's ups-and-downs. The tribulations of pregnancy, illness, unemployment, old age and death, were, in a sense, predictable; that being so, it must surely be obvious that frugality and foresight should prevail and that men should save against harder times ahead. In fact, working people did save. By the last quarter of the century, 8 million people were investing in Friendly Societies of various kinds. But – and this was the nub of the problem which philanthropists failed to address – what was to be done for those who could not save? What of those people, armies of them, whose wages, even when in regular employment, were inadequate to survive? What good was the incentive to save to those with no surplus cash at the end of an arduous week's work?

By the 1880s, doubts had become widespread, especially in educated circles, that philanthropy as widely practised was no real solution to the nation's poverty. These were the years, as contemporaries noted, of a heightened conscience about social matters. At this time embryonic socialist movements began to address the same issues, with different solutions of course. There was a resurgence of literature, passionate and socially aware, which raised new questions and made new proposals for improving social conditions. One such was the establishment of 'settlements' of graduates in poorer urban communities. These may have done little for the poor, but they proved a remarkable experience for a number of young men, who went on to be pioneering social reformers in the twentieth century. The first Fabian pamphlet, published in 1884, was entitled *Why are the Many Poor?* Politicians and newspaper commentators, of varying political hues and discomforted by contemporary revelations, had begun to change their views in the last twenty years of the century.

At Christmas 1894 the *Manchester Guardian* intoned: 'the world must be made a better place for the underprivileged many.' Not since the early years of Victoria's reign, during the Chartist turmoil, had so much attention been paid in print to the wretchedness of the British people, and the radical upheavals which might flow from it. British socialism, unlike its European partners, was still undeveloped and no match for the existing party structures, which were themselves newly responsive to the widening of British democracy, particularly after the 1884 Reform Act. Many wished to deny it the fertile breeding ground manifest in British cities. So by the last years of Victoria's reign, the nation's philanthropic movement faced new and more intractable problems. More than that, it became clear beyond any refutation that charity alone could never help large numbers of the poor.

These were the years when a modern democracy came into being in Britain, excepting of course for women. The political parties began to reorganise themselves on the understanding that the electorate's voice had to be heeded. Constituency organisations developed, in both the main Conservative and Liberal parties, and organised labour began those preliminary moves which were to create the Labour party early in the twentieth century. Not surprisingly, politicians of all persuasions turned to the question of poverty, and the failure of philanthropy to stop it, as a major issue which was important in itself, but would also be likely to prove electorally attractive to a more widely democratic and sensitive electorate. Politicians were merely raising an issue which was a recurring theme in popular print in the 1880s.

The discussion of poverty was in part a result of a down-turn in the economy in the 1870s: the 'Great Depression' which has attracted so much historical controversy. After more than half a century of industrial growth, there were limits to what the economy could achieve; and there were layers of the population which remained untouched by the material benefits of industrial growth. The consequent contrast between prosperity and poverty caught the eye, and the attention of writers keen to explain it. Popular articles in the press, major investigative landmarks like George's *Poverty and Progress* (1881) and Mearn's *The Bitter Cry of Outcast London* (1883), revitalised concern about the urban poor and about the failure of all the efforts of philanthropists to reduce the problem. To make matters worse, large-scale Russian and Polish Jewish immigration began into the very worst of urban communities, London's East End and elsewhere. The poor descended upon the poor.

Many thought the answer lay overseas, in those areas of the globe being actively settled by the British. Thus, from 1880 to 1914 emigration schemes loomed large in a number of proposals devoted to solving British urban poverty. Cecil Rhodes approved; so too did General Booth, founder of the Salvation Army. Perhaps surprisingly, so did some early socialists. Others thought it more appropriate to point to the contemporary philanthropy devoted to native peoples in the empire, and the prevailing levels of domestic poverty there. Was this, again, another example of British 'telescopic philanthropy', a concern for the miseries of native peoples while neglecting the plight of the British poor? This had been an argument which had raged since the 1820s, when the campaigns against slavery had regularly been accused of diverting charitable interest, by ignoring domestic issues in favour of the condition of slaves in the West Indies. In answer it could scarcely be claimed that domestic life lacked its fair share of charitable effort. The fact remained that it was not the amount of charity at home which was at fault; it was its failure to achieve results.

This, then, was the central issue to be grasped from the profusion of literature and political argument about poverty from the 1880s onwards. Charity had made scarcely a dent in urban poverty. With this in mind, what was to be said for the view, so pronounced within the ranks of the COS, that moral or personal failings were the cause of poverty? What signs were there of that moral elevation so vital if individuals were to be able to raise themselves from the mire of urban poverty? In fact the true situation was doubly alarming, for revelations about poverty were paralleled by revelations about dreadful levels of 'moral' and physical degradation – of child prostitution and widespread physical debility among the young, for instance. Contemporary intellectual fads, notably the eugenics and early social science movement, made great play with these failings. An intellectual climate evolved in which 'race' had become a key social and human category, and late Victorians came increasingly to consider their own society, and the world at large, sub-divided into 'race' rather than 'class'. The evidence available to them from the year 1880 suggested that, despite their heroic charitable efforts, the British 'race' was being progressively weakened by the wretchedness of life for millions of its poor.

It was at this point that Charles Booth began his detailed researches into poverty in the East End of London. It proved to be a remarkable project, its impact matched by its scope and size. In seventeen volumes published between 1889 and 1903, Booth and his team of researchers laid waste most of the existing theories and ideas about the urban poor. Most devastating of all was his central point that something close to one-third of the capital's population lived on, or close to, 'the poverty line'. How could mere charity hope to deal with poverty on such a scale? Before Booth had finished his last volume, Seebohm Rowntree, in his York study, had confirmed its main drift: that upwards of a third of the people were poor. As Rowntree concluded:

We are faced by the startling probability that from 25 to 30 per cent of the town populations of the United Kingdom are living in poverty.

To what benefit therefore had been the prodigious expenditure of Victorian charity in the face of this awful truth? What possible long-term hope could philanthropy extend to the poor? Clearly, there were millions of Victorians whose material lives had been eased a little by charitable work; food, clothing, shelter and care had regularly come the way of the towns' most abject citizens. But was this to be the prospect for a third of the people in the new twentieth century? Were they and their offspring, like their parents and grandparents before them, to be able to endure those periodic hardships of life thanks only to the goodwill and the efforts of their more prosperous contemporaries?

What made the bleak prospects facing the poor all the more unacceptable was the changing social and political climate. The British attachment to charity had not had its day, in fact the late twentieth century was to witness even more spectacular examples of British philanthropy, but it was abundantly clear to most people that charity alone could not provide an acceptable solution to the nation's most pressing domestic concern. Politicians looked abroad, to countries such as New Zealand and Germany, and saw a different way of attempting to mitigate social ills. Tories, Liberals and labour leaders began seriously to propose the state itself as the only obvious and adequate guardian of the people's material and social well-being. No one could possible claim that the commitment to social reform had begun to carry all before it – or even to carry the support of a majority of the nation's politicians. By 1901, however, it had clearly been placed on the political agenda. And to a degree this had come about through the indisputable and demonstrable failure of one of the most impressive of Victorian values – the attachment to charity as an instrument of social policy. Like so many Victorian values, charity had been shown to be of only marginal value to its recipients.

9

PRIDE IN
TOWN AND COUNTRY

LATE Victorians were fond of celebrating their attachment to, and pride in, their native region. Expressions of civic pride and national fervour were frequent among the British in the late nineteenth century. The parades and festivals in most towns, the more colourful and explosive outbursts of collective patriotism at moments of military victory or royal celebrations, seem, in retrospect, to have been essentially Victorian. That they were the product of the Victorian age is true to an unexpected degree, for many of the aspects of civic and patriotic pride which were bequeathed to the twentieth century were, in large part, artificial traditions invented by Victorians, and yet soon thought of as basic and historically-shaped features of British life since time out of mind. The British are famous for their traditions; they ought to be equally famous for inventing or transforming many of them and passing them off as the fruits of historical continuity. Scottish dress, Welsh Eisteddfods, the English devotion to their monarchy – all have common ingredients of artificiality. Yet, having been invented, they endured, prospered, and eventually took their place in the pantheon of ancient British traditions.

The attachment to place and nation was not peculiar to the Victorians. It became a feature of European history throughout the nineteenth century. It is also true that similar responses could be found at earlier periods. Yet Victorian life saw the transformation of older allegiances into newer, different and often more passionate attachments. Even then, it is easy to overstate these feelings, and to forget that while this collective pride in locality and nation was the dominant mood, there existed a contrary, resistant feeling.

Pride in locality had been a feature of British life for centuries, though the focus for such activities tended to be largely parochial. It was around the local customs of the parish – rush bearings, beating the bounds, harvest customs, village games, dancing, wakes – that a cycle of local acts of identity was performed. The more robust expressions of such parochial enjoyments tended to be the preserve of men – in particular healthy young men. The concept of a 'local derby', for instance, derives from an ancient game of football played annually between the young men of rival parishes in the town of Derby. Such occasions, in the words of Keith Wrightson, 'punctuated the calendar of the working year and reaffirmed in merriment the neighbourly ties and collective identity which could be of vital importance to the physical and emotional security of individuals and families'. This world was under severe attack at the accession of Victoria. The popular culture of the pre-industrial world was out of kilter with the needs and rhythms of the new industrial and urban society. Early Victorians often bemoaned the erosion and death of community-based popular culture. 'A mighty revolution has taken place in the sports and pastimes of the common people,' wrote one man in 1840. A little later, another remarked that 'The few remnants of our old Sports and Pastimes are rapidly disappearing and this is, in my opinion, a change much to be lamented.' We know that many survived throughout the century. Nonetheless, it is generally true that these celebrations which had shaped people's feelings towards their local community were greatly altered by the changes in early Victorian society. It was to repair the consequent damage to local attachments that new popular cultures emerged to express that sense of collective local feeling.

As towns changed, so too did people's attachment to them. Older, more turbulent expressions of local feeling were brought under control by a combination of laws, new policing, and the new discipline of an urban people. Local rivalries were decreasingly physical and aggressive. Instead they took on a more amenable, disciplined form. The popular culture of local life was as peaceful as its predecessor had been turbulent. Parishes and towns remained in competition with each other, but it was, by and large, a peaceable tradition. Brass band contests, football games, choral festivals – these and others absorbed and re-channeled the old traditions of local pride and imposed on them a peaceable style more in keeping with the social tone of late Victorian life.

For many people their localities were alien places. The migration of people into the towns, from the countryside or from Ireland, meant that, initially at least, there was little sense of local pride among substantial numbers of Victorian town-dwellers. Often, instead, they transplanted their own rural, or national, attachments to the towns. In time, however, and notwithstanding continuing migrations, local loyalties developed among the next generation. Among immigrants and natives, the cultivation of local attachments came about primarily by belonging to organisations and institutions which actively fostered a sense of community. From factory or workshop, chapel or church, Sunday school, place of learning, local pub or place of recreation, there emerged a sense of local loyalty which was sometimes much more specific than pride in the local town. When viewed together, they created a broad cultural landscape whose focus was the locality, bounded by the local residence, workplace, church and place of recreation. In a sense, it was almost like the pre-industrial loyalties to the local parish. But by the late nineteenth century it was secular rather than religious in its shape and organisation. Thus within the expanding towns and cities of late Victorian life, there was a mosaic of local loyalties and pride, much of it expressed through the medium of popular culture.

What gave such feelings a 'modern' look was the new transport systems and the rapid development of recreational competition as a way of late nineteenth-century life. Urban transport systems, but more especially the national railway network, enabled local groups to travel and compete against their peers in other towns and cities. Historians have tended, rightly, to view this as the key element in the spread of national recreations. But it was also crucial in generating competition between far-flung localities and creating a consequent rivalry between towns, regions and communities. Again, this was generally conducted through popular culture. Teams, bands, choirs, with their followers, took to the trains to compete or support; they paraded their local pride before their opponents and asserted the superiority of their home town over that of their opponents. Sometimes such rivalries were traditional and were now merely given a new garb. In the main, however, they were new and distinctive, expressions of pride in a particular town whose representatives were competing with another town. It was a process greatly promoted by the rapid growth of a local press which gave much coverage to, and actively encouraged, local pride and the activities of local groups. After 1880 this growing attachment to local town was further encouraged by compulsory schooling, in which the virtues of civic pride became part of a broader social education. Children learnt to take a pride in their home town and in their nation.

On top of these changes there developed a new form of local pride, encouraged by local men of substance, often politicians, keen to promote local attachments for their own purpose. As part of the creation of local traditions (or the revival of old, neglected traditions), politicians placed great emphasis – and often a lot of money – on community projects, buildings and celebrations. Civic buildings were the most dramatic of such investments; town halls and municipal offices were built on the most lavish of scales, in emulation of the more venerable buildings of older cities. They were a monument not only to the well-being and confidence of the men who built them, but to their pride and attachment to the town. To accompany those buildings, there developed a parallel tradition of civic pageantry. Whenever national or local events demanded it, mayors, aldermen, elected representatives and officials bedecked themselves in their new-found fineries and insignia of office, and paraded round the town. In a sense there was nothing new in this. Ancient cities and organisations, the law, guilds, local freemen and the like, had long traditions of pageantry and ceremonial. In part it was an essential element in the exercise, conferment or acceptance of power; ceremonies designed to impress the public with the power or awesomeness of the law, or to legitimise local government. But not to be outdone, local politicians in the 'new' towns of the nineteenth century invariably copied these colourful panoplies of office. Chains of office, a mace, gowns, hoods, colourful attire of all sorts – these and more added a splendid gloss to the more mundane exercise of local political power. They also offered, when paraded regularly through the streets, an expression of local pride and an opportunity for the onlooker to share in that sentiment. Even in the meanest and most blighted of new towns, such trappings of local high office, accompanied of course by the ranks of clergy, uniformed police, firemen and local bands, offered a dash of spectacular colour which inspired a sense of awe and pride in the locality.

By the last quarter of the nineteenth century, the British had developed a sense of communal and civic attachment. It was most colourfully expressed in the set-piece parades to mark royal jubilees, military victories or even a minor local occasion. At Colchester the civic 'oyster feast', from being a simple civic meal in the early nineteenth century, developed between 1880 and 1914 into a lavish display of civic pride, when hundreds of guests from 'all classes of society in the borough and neighbourhood' dined at the mayor's expense. There were other self-conscious efforts at the cultivation of local pride and attachment to community. They were of course only one element, albeit the most colourful, in the complex development of local loyalties. By Victoria's death, there could be no doubt of the scale, importance and ubiquity of pride in one's town or city. The British were a nation of town dwellers: they had also begun to register relatively new loyalty to those towns. But some might feel that many of them had little to be thankful or proud of.

Joseph Chamberlain is the man regularly cited as the politician who sought both to inculcate local civic pride and to make the city responsive to the needs of the inhabitants. Chamberlain was Mayor of Birmingham between 1873 and 1875, pioneered slum clearance in that city and became the most famous spokesman for 'gas and water socialism' – the municipal control over basic amenities. In Birmingham, profits from such ventures were invested in art galleries and libraries rather than into private hands. Yet Chamberlain was only the most famous of such entrepreneurs, largely because of his subsequent career at Westminster. More typical of the local politician was that breed of men whose new-found wealth was rooted in local economic activity, like Chamberlain's, but whose political horizons did not stretch beyond the city boundary. Indeed it was these very qualities which proved so important in cultivating local civic pride. Society's older elites, from landed rural society, tended to shun local city or town politics. So too did men who were 'socially or intellectually eminent'. Local council politics were an increasingly demanding business, subject by the 1880s to vexatious party disciplines. To an older elite, schooled in a more leisurely style of life, such controls and limitations were irksome. There were more attractive outlets for their energies and free time, in rural life and rural government, and of course at Westminster. The result was that, in general, urban government fell under the control and influence of local business interests, often of self-made men. Their status was clearly enhanced by the trappings of local office; established elites were unlikely to feel themselves improved by being mayor or alderman of an unattractive town. The end result of this process, the emergence of local business groups into high local political office, was that men of often fierce local attachments governed these towns. These were men whose status, wealth and future were rooted in and nurtured by the local community.

By and large, the city fathers of late Victorian Britain were proud of their community. In 1887 the mayor of Middlesborough told the

Prince of Wales, there to open the new town hall, that the town's blanket of smoke was 'an indication of plenty of work'. A Birmingham man made a similar point, arguing that views of the Swiss Alps did not thrill him as much as the view 'when I have looked down on the smoky streets of Birmingham from the railway'. These were men proud to admit the ties between muck and money; and they were equally proud of their achievements in the community in creating local prosperity. It was quite natural that they should go to such lengths to further pride in their communities. Thus the changing politics of local government was itself partly responsible for promoting that feeling of local pride, of attachment to community, that distinguished the late years of Victoria's reign. It was a different loyalty from anything known before in British history; it was essentially Victorian.

Perhaps the most abiding images of late Victorian life are those associated with the achievements of empire, and the British people's apparent delight in those achievements. It is widely assumed that the British were deeply patriotic – at certain moments excessively so. Yet there are qualifications to be made to this image. There were certain obvious periods when patriotism flared into public display. In wartime, at moments of imperial conquest or crisis and, towards the end of the reign, at certain royal celebrations, the British did indeed take to the streets to celebrate. But at less spectacular moments, the people's attachment to their nation tended to be of a different order. Similarly, the popularity of the monarch was not always high, notably in the earlier part of Victoria's reign. Yet the images of monarchy and empire, and the widespread support for both, remain among the clearest images of Victorian life.

It is not surprising that in wartime people expressed their patriotism more fully than in peacetime. Yet compared to the eighteenth or twentieth centuries, Victorian life was relatively untroubled by major wars. Victoria's reign had been begun only twenty-four years after the ending of the French Wars which had raged with only a brief interval between 1793 and 1815. In those years, and despite flurries of anti-war feeling, patriotic outbursts had punctuated the wars. Under Victoria however, the most serious wars were those of the Crimea (1854–55) and, at the end of her reign, the Boer War. Wartime apart, the British army was relatively small and not very popular – a result primarily of the cost of keeping an army, and a long-standing distrust of 'standing armies'.

This began to change in the 1870s, when Cardwell's reforms re-organised the army, and put the regimental structure on a local basis. This had the effect of tapping local pride and attachments and encouraging local loyalty in the appropriate regiment. But it was a policy which was to prove utterly disastrous in World War I, when a regiment's heavy losses meant a grievous blow to its home town or county. The army became accomplished at colonial wars, at defeating native peoples and aiding the grab for empire. Its largest forces were in India where, the Great Mutiny of 1857 apart, it was thought to be the successful tool in conquest and civilisation. Similarly in Egypt, the Sudan and, later, black Africa, the army was the instrument of relatively successful British conquest and expansion. But the limitations of the army, of the tactics, training and manpower, were not fully revealed until the disasters of the Boer War. It was then, when 450,000 men were poured into Lord Roberts' army, and when military and political fortunes were mixed, that the British began to celebrate in earnest their military achievements. Often, it was celebration heightened by relief at the narrow escapes from disaster. Not for the last time, the British were to take delight not so much in winning, but in escaping from disaster.

By the end of Victoria's reign the language and tone of British patriotism was decidedly to the right of British politics. Yet we need to be reminded that a century earlier, the language of patriotism had been closely identified with radicalism and opposition. The 'Free-Born Englishman' and his radical movements regarded themselves as the repositories of the country's true identity against a usurping and authoritarian state, anxious to curb traditional liberties. By and large the argument about patriotism (and the word 'patriotic' was often used to described radicals) tended to be part of a domestic British political debate; of reformers versus a resistant and corrupt political system. But from the 1840s the language of patriotism began to change. By 1870 patriotism had become an element on the right, not the radical wing, of politics. Conservatism, thanks in part to Disraeli's overt use of patriotism, began to l···e middle and working-class support. Throughout the 1870s Britain's role in the world, and especially in the Mediterranean, became an issue of major political importance. By 1880 patriotism had shaded into a form of jingoism which was to be a feature of British life until World War I. Patriotism was henceforth used as a political tool, a demand that everyone should be loyal, not to sectional interests but to the state. It became a powerful weapon in the hands of these at the apex of national authority.

What gave this patriotic phenomenon such power was its association with empire. As the empire grew in size, and as military exploits added to the empire and to the list of British conquests, a fiercely expressed patriotism became more pronounced and more broadly based. Two forces proved important in this development: firstly, the coming of compulsory schooling and the importance attached to the lessons of empire; and secondly, a widely literate British people were assailed on all sides by the new press, the popular dailies and weeklies to which empire and military ventures were the stuff of mass circulation. The literature of childhood, the lessons in school, the press of adult life, all contributed to a powerful cultivation of an imperial mood. And all of this was quite apart from the patriotic promptings to be picked up in society at large; in the new arena of party politics, popular culture (notably the music hall), in games and religion. In a society given over increasingly to a national mood of patriotism, it was difficult for people to resist or remain impervious to this climate.

Despite a barrage of patriotic fervour, patriotism was not always a successful political weapon. Those who sought to make political capital from it sometimes failed. Even in the 'Khaki election' of 1900 (a General Election dominated by the Boer war), the issue failed to yield the political returns expected of it. Equally, it is not clear that the jingoistic songs in the music hall evoked any important or durable patriotic feelings in the audience. They clearly expressed and reflected a particular mood and could, at certain critical times, elicit a fierce popular response. But these emotions were normally brief and fleeting. Nor does the voluntary military recruitment of young men tell us much about popular patriotism. The great bulk of those who tried to join the army, like the great bulk rejected on medical grounds, came from humbler homes and communities where regular work and wages were hard to find. It was necessity, not patriotism, which drove most working-class youths and men towards the army. This is not to claim that they lacked patriotism or that they were indifferent to the prevailing social mood. But it seems likely that the more exaggerated moods and expressions of patriotism were much less striking in daily plebeian life than much of the evidence might suggest. The spasms of public patriotic rejoicings passed quickly, the glories of empire and warfare gave way to more immediate needs and worries.

This is not to argue however that patriotism was either a 'false' sentiment or had no importance or meaning. It would be wrong to claim that these flashes of patriotism represented no more than the manipulative influence of politicians and press, keen and able to whip up popular feeling. There were, obviously, millions of Britons who had cause to take a great pride in their nation and its achievements, even when they themselves seemed to have little or nothing to show for it. But the nature of patriotism itself changed in the nineteenth century. The early nineteenth-century patriotism of opposition and of radical politics had been transformed into that late-century variant which was conservative, right-wing, and deeply influenced by ideas of racial superiority.

What lay behind much of the popular patriotism of the late century was a firm belief in British superiority. At the heart of that belief lay complex ideas about race and racial inferiority. Towards the end of Victoria's reign, the British had come to accept that, in the racial hierarchy of mankind, they stood supreme. In part, they had only to look at their empire, at the variety of races and peoples they governed, to find apparent confirmation of this view. But, like the development of Victorian patriotism, the related sense of racial superiority was not a 'natural' phenomenon but had emerged from specific, and sometimes surprising, nineteenth-century forces.

There had been elements of racial thinking at an earlier phase of empire, notably in India and in the Caribbean slave islands. But the campaigns to end the slave trade and slavery had inaugurated a different, quite new, intellectual mood, when briefly a benign attitude towards non-whites had prevailed. This was rapidly dispelled in the 1850s and 1860s, both as a result of major colonial troubles (the Indian Mutiny and the Morant Bay revolt in Jamaica in 1865) and by the parallel development of anthropological and 'scientific' racism. There emerged a powerful belief that the 'races' of the world were divided by fundamental anatomical and intellectual differences, that some were destined to be led by others. Naturally enough the British were held to be superior, a belief reinforced by the sense that their institutions, of law, politics, indeed civilisation, were similarly superior to all others in the world. Destined by racial superiority to govern and to lead, the British were doubly blessed by the unquestioned and unequalled excellence of their institutions. It was thus an obligation imposed by the Almighty on the British to bestow their superior way of life on native peoples throughout the world. Large numbers of Victorians genuinely held such views, and our retrospective awareness of the cruder realities of empire can in no way diminish the strength of Victorian convictions. Such views made straight the way to imperial conquest. But they were not a mere cover, a smoke screen, for economic interests.

Mid-Victorians, however, had certain intellectual doubts about the composition, the make-up, of the people of Britain itself. Intellectuals argued about the British 'national character'. Some argued for a varied human composition which included the Celtic fringes and suggested that the British were a polyglot rather than a single 'race'. Among proponents of this argument was Matthew Arnold, whose book, *The Study of Celtic Literature*, was envisaged as 'a major effort to determine the Celtic component of the English national character'. Pitched against this view however was the 'Teutonic' school – led notably by Charles Kingsley and Anthony Froude – which argued that the British 'race' had a single base. For them, as for many other observers of urban Britain, overseas expansion and settlement offered a solution to the dire physical problems of Britain's poor urban masses. By the time the British were poised to embark on a new and even more expansive phase of empire, into Africa, the belief had gained support that the British were, *tout court*, a 'race', able and duty-bound to dominate the world's lesser breeds.

There were important cross-currents and conflicts in the intellectual discussion and analysis of 'race' between 1880 and 1914 and beyond, and it would be false to suggest that there was only one simple view of race or racial hierarchy. This was compounded by the political and intellectual crisis created by the Boer War. Doubts had begun to undermine faith in the British imperial mission. At Victoria's death, this tended to be a rather subdued debate among a minority. More obvious was that assertive national pride in empire and civilisation which had been the political and intellectual descant to the main imperial refrain for the past quarter of a century. At its heart was a strident belief in the superiority of the British, and the inferiority of non-white peoples. To call this view racist is not to indulge in present-day political jargon. It is merely descriptive, a simple, factual account of a view of the world which saw mankind designated and ordered into degrees of superiority or inferiority by the accident of race. Thus when the British indulged in their periodic outbursts of patriotism, they were celebrating the achievements not only of their armies, their statesmen or their economy, but also of their race.

There is, however, a distinct paradox here, for, at the moment of pride in the achievements of the British 'race', there was growing concern about the problems of the 'lesser breeds' in British cities. Pride in empire and overseas settlement was tempered by worry about the degeneration of the British race at home. Thus empire and domestic life were closely linked; the one was the polar opposite of the other. What was the point, the virtue, in empire if the lot of millions of the urban poor remained abject and depressing? Moreover, the eugenics movement and the popularisation of its findings suggested that the British 'race' faced a process of cumulative racial degeneration; the ill-nourished poor bequeathed their physical and mental deficiencies to their large numbers of offspring. Somehow or other, an escape route needed to be devised in this ever-downward spiral of 'racial' degeneration. One answer, or rather a complex series of answers, took the form of a more thorough-going social policy, supervised and financed by the state. This solution was advocated not only by reformers. There were prominent imperialists equally anxious to reform life at home, if only to strengthen the domestic foundations of the world's greatest imperial nation. Yet at the heart of this welter of views about Britain's present and future role in the world there lay an indisputable fact – a fierce pride in and attachment to the achievements of the nation. Late Victorian patriotism was, as we have seen, complex; but it was a major force, ubiquitous in that it embraced all classes, and subtly persuasive, even among those with apparently little to show or gain from it.

This patriotism formed a chorus of approval for, in retrospect, some of Britain's more dubious international ventures. It was a creed which was generally aggressive and domineering. Late Victorian patriotism, whether in its more cultivated or its more popular form, prided itself in the relegation and subjection of native peoples, their cultures and beliefs. Similarly, in promoting an expansive and dominating attachment to British values of the time, it sought to lay waste the cultures of other peoples. It is no task of the historian to blame Victorians for espousing this fierce patriotism; it was a historical fact, a major force in the lives of millions of late Victorians. Is it, however, a force worthy of revival? Is it in any way pertinent to British life a century later? There are many qualities and achievements of British life which readily spring to mind as worthy candidates for collective admiration. But what purpose would be served by exhuming the remains of ideas, designed to function in the world of our great-grandparents, but of dubious relevance to a post-imperial and economically contracting nation? Victorian patriotism was, after all, not a universal value but, rather, specific to that limited, historical epoch. Its values and usefulness was to die with the end of the empire.

IO

PRUDERY AND
PERMISSIVENESS

IT is hard to think of any aspect of Victorian life that has been
more comprehensively misunderstood, and misrepresented, than
sexuality. This is true not merely of the broader public, understandably unfamiliar with the details of Victorian life, but also of
large numbers of historians, many of whom have been happy to
repeat the received ideas of Victorian sexuality. Indeed the word
'Victorian' has itself come to be used, like 'Puritan', to describe a
set of moral and sexual values which seem, to many, to have been
odd and even bizarre. Prudery, a repugnance for sexual contact,
the denial of female sexual pleasure, cold functional sexual relations inside the bourgeois marriage, complemented for men by
necessary liaisons with mistresses or prostitutes, comical efforts to
mask public sexuality and nudity – these form part of a perception
of Victorian life which has served in large part to distort the reality.
It is not so much that these attitudes were untrue but that they may
have been untypical, unrepresentative, which needs to be stressed.
For every sexually joyless marriage, how many more were eroti-
cally satisfactory; for every nude sculpture draped, how many
onlookers thought it ridiculous; how many women accorded to the
advice not to succumb to sexual pleasure? Yet time and again, in
both professional and popular circles, the old caricatured images
are repeated, persistently presented as if they were indisputable
gospel.

More recently, in Britain and North America, these images of
Victorian life have proved doubly attractive to those powerful
bodies of opinion which see them as a blessed and healthy state of
grace before the fall into sexual licence (and even depravity) of
recent decades. Victorian sexuality in its restrained, controlled,
unhistorical form is now offered as an antidote to the sexual licence
which appears to have descended on the western world. Better the

prudery of Victorian life than the corrosive permissiveness of the past quarter of a century. And almost as if to bring proof of the argument, the ravage of a new deadly epidemic has begun to blight the world; proof to those who need it of the medical and even divine reactions to the sins of an indulgent society. For any historian of Victorian life, it is hard to reconcile the alleged ubiquity and pervasiveness of sexual repression with the remarkable achievements of that age; if Victorians had been the 'emotional cripples' so often alleged, it is hard to explain their achievements at home and abroad. Recent work, notably by Peter Gay, has thoroughly demolished the idea that Victorians were sexually repressed. Some Victorians, naturally enough, were, or were for some of the time. But to imagine that, in talking of Victorian life, we are dealing with a thoroughly sexually-repressed society, one in which sexuality was comprehensively denied, is quite wrong.

Examples to the contrary could be cited in abundance; in the words of Peter Gay, of 'impotent husbands, frigid wives, young men and women innocent of the most elementary facts of life; and scandalous reports of homosexual establishments or the illicit traffic in prepubertial girls . . .' But similar examples could be cited from throughout the western world in the 1980s. Then, as now, such cases provide not so much typical, representative examples of a repressed or warped sexuality, but of elements in an extraordinarily rich mosaic of sexual behaviour and attitudes. There was, in Peter Gay's opinion, within that bourgeois culture which determined these images of Victorian sexuality, conflicts, ambivalence and diversity. Victorian life was characterised, according to Jeffrey Weeks, not by a fixed set of standards and moral certainties, but by conflicts between contrasting beliefs and behaviour; between 'different classes and regions, religious, racial and ethnic groups'. There was, in brief,

> no Golden Age of sexual propriety, and the search for it in the mythologised past tells us more about present confusions than past glories.

Much of the modern social and medical debate about sexuality originated in the nineteenth century. The terms homosexuality and lesbianism were invented in that century; Victorian doctors paid increasing attention to the physiology, and later the psychology, of sexuality, while broader issues such as illegitimacy, prostitution and the 'age of consent' were topics of major public and political debate. There is plenty of evidence, from the private or public lives of Victorians, to suggest that sex was a mentionable topic. This is not to claim that everyone was prepared to discuss it openly. And it is at this point that we confront one of the most extraordinary misinterpretations of Victorian life. It has been widely assumed that the Victorian reluctance or failure to discuss, privately or publicly, certain areas of sexuality is evidence of a sexual problem, a repression or denial of sexual feelings. Yet reticence about sex was not particularly Victorian, or uniquely bourgeois. In a late twentieth-century western world, in which openness and exposing one's most personal sexual or psychological features has become commonplace, it is often difficult to recall that reticence on such matters was normal, and natural. Only in a society influenced by the babble of sexuality does reticence seem odd.

The Victorian hesitation to speak or write about sexual matters was part of a long tradition of delicacy about behaviour which was, and is, highly personal. Nor was it peculiar to the supposedly inhibited middle class. Research on working-class autobiographies has amply demonstrated the reluctance of working men to describe their innermost emotions. Much of the problem was vocabulary. Which words, expressions, could capture the feelings of love and sexuality? Often the popular vernacular sufficed: 'I was as fond of my wife as a Cat is of New Milk.' Often, a suitable word or expression was hard to find, and 'codes' were used; but this was, and is, true about the language of bodily functions. Ignorance of anatomy, the arcane language of biology and the dependence of many people upon their own coded variants and vernacular will not, in themselves, provide clues to sexual attitudes. Yet there was often no need to express such feelings, and it is a dangerous historical game of reconstruction to impute to people in the past certain psychological problems on the basis of their silence. Silence may have been golden but it was not of necessity an indication of sexual ambivalence.

Victorians were often far from being reluctant to talk about sex, albeit indirectly. Indeed, many of the issues already discussed in this book had obvious sexual dimensions. Questions about population growth, illegitimacy, prostitution – that range of problems brought into focus by the growth of a densely-crowded urban society – were high on the Victorian political agenda. Parliamentary scrutiny of working conditions in mines and factories in the 1830s and 1840s returned frequently to the question of sexuality. Often, of course, questions of sex were debated behind the veneer of moral issues – such as that of domestic overcrowding. In the

1860s, there was widespread discussion of sexuality, notably of prostitution and venereal disease, in the arguments which culminated in the Contagious Diseases Acts. These Acts, which involved enforced medical inspection of suspected prostitutes in military towns, not only marked a major step forward in the arbitrary power of the state over the individual, but were, partly for that reason, fiercely resisted. In the fifteen years to 1885, more than 2½ million people signed 17,367 petitions against the Acts, and more than 900 public meetings were called against them. Abolitionists produced 520 books and pamphlets to advance their case. This hardly suggests public reticence in debating sexual matters.

In newspapers, magazines and books, sexual matters were freely and openly discussed, often in a salacious style familiar today. Scandalous divorces, sexual incidents of all sorts, found abundant coverage in mid and late-Victorian print. Pornography, different from today's variety in that it was primarily printed rather than pictorial, was not only available but provides some telling insights into Victorian life. In the fantasies of the Victorian pornographer, lower-class women, especially servants and country girls, and even children, figure as the objects of primarily middle and upper-class male desires. Science began to create its own vocabulary for the varied physical and psychological aspects of sexuality, in a literature which, if obviously specialised, nonetheless passed into common parlance by being incorporated into English dictionaries. How are we to reconcile such evidence, most of it from the world of the propertied Victorian, with the popular images of Victorian bourgeois prudery? Does one set of evidence cancel out the other, or is it, more reasonably perhaps, to be integrated alongside it, providing a contrasting mosaic of attitudes and forms of behaviour?

A major difficulty in comprehending Victorian sexuality was the role of the family or, more precisely, the propaganda generated by various proponents of certain ideals of family life. As with much Victorian propaganda, the evidence from those sources has loomed inordinately large in recent assessments of Victorian life. The nuclear family which formed the basic unit of British life had been in place for centuries past. But in the nineteenth century the bourgeois family spawned numerous defenders and critics: those who saw it as the source of all individual and collective good, and those who imputed to it a host of contemporary ailments. Towards the end of the century, Freud began to blame its Viennese variant for a number of his patients' sexual problems. The family was the prime agency of socialising the people; it taught them their social and sex roles, their disciplines and relationships, their values and attachments. It often failed. Similarly, it sought to embrace those bereft of family; the orphaned young for whom artificial families, inside or outside institutions, were invented. To many, the nineteenth-century middle-class family was the key to that refinement of manners so noticeable as the years advanced. According to John Stuart Mill,

> The association of men and women in daily life is much closer and more complete than it ever was before. Men's life is more domestic . . .

Civilisation, the revulsion against rougher amusements, a growing sense of duty, all 'have thrown the man very much more upon home and its inmates, for his personal and social pleasures'. It was this image of the domestic bourgeois ideal which dominated the literature, and iconography, of Victorian family life. It was a patriarchal unit, dominated in reality no less than in the ideal by the husband. The law confirmed the male's pre-eminence. But this is not to deny the hidden realities: the key role of women in child-rearing and educating, in managing domestics and budgeting. In fact the importance of the woman in the family can be gauged by the speed with which widowers re-married; they simply needed another helpmate in the complex ordering and management of family life.

The man dominated, even though his role may have been subverted by his wife's labours and economic wealth; he was the source of discipline, even when in fact it was administered by his spouse. It was a role imposed upon him by divine providence, an obligation not merely to his wife and offspring but also to the Almighty. It was equally incumbent on the woman to obey the source of authority. Again, this was confirmed by the law which severely limited married women's control over their own property and finance; their rights were subsumed within those of their husbands. This was a paradoxical role, for the woman was the pillar upon which family life was based. But, in the plethora of manuals and guidebooks published for such women, that role was rarely viewed as an equal one. In practice matters were often different. Women turned to other women for advice and succour, notably in working-class communities. They performed all the complex economic and social tasks which made family and social life possible. They were, in many respects, clearly the equals of their menfolk –

but not in law, and not within the pages of the literature of bourgeois domesticity.

Much the same was true in sexual relations. Firstly, it was an issue which few spoke about because then, as now, it was an issue which concerned no one else. Yet if it was the woman's duty to obey, this is not to claim that women were the mere passive objects of their spouses' sexual desires. Certainly a great deal of medical opinion held that women could not enjoy sexual encounters. It is also true that most middle and upper-class women were woefully ignorant about sex when they married. Annie Besant married 'with no more idea of the marriage relation than if I had been four years old instead of twenty'. Judged by modern standards of sex education, the great majority of Victorians, men and women, appear to have been remarkably ignorant about sex. This is not to say that they had not picked up that folklore of sex, from siblings, friends and others, which might have gone some way towards remedying the omissions of parents. Even the Queen had simply advised her eldest daughter in 1859 that women were 'born for man's pleasure and amusement'. Yet it would be wrong to claim that, because of this absence of sexual education, Victorian women were unable to enjoy their married sex lives. It is true enough that many found their initial sexual encounters perplexing and shocking; whether they developed into more satisfactory relations is more difficult to assess. There is evidence, however, of a satisfactory sexuality where we might not expect it. A late-century sample of 45 middle-class American women by a doctor showed that 33 had experienced sexual desire and the majority had experienced orgasm. It would be wrong to imagine that the severe conventions of bourgeois life actually inhibited or prevented sexual fulfilment.

Female sexuality was assumed to take place within the confines of the family; but this had also been true for centuries. It was equally applicable to menfolk, though they, unlike their wives, had opportunities of sexual encounters outside marriage; the degree to which they took up these opportunities is unclear, and presumably varied enormously. But it would be bizarre to imagine that, in general, men were forced into the arms of mistresses and prostitutes because of the frigidity of the bourgeois married woman. Some doubtless were; many were not.

The subservience of women was clearly underlined by the enormous difficulties they faced if they cast aside the roles expected of them. The concept of the 'fallen woman' was no mere evangelical image; it was a fate imposed upon thousands of women by a society unwilling to tolerate, in public, free or 'errant' sexual ways among women. Single women with a child suffered the worst of society's punishments; ostracised and shunned, denied a place in the lying-in wards, such women endured the worst ravages of infant mortality and they themselves died in childbirth at a far higher rate than any other group. Women who left their husbands, however justified, found their lives socially and economically difficult in the extreme. Pioneering families, promoting relations other than the marital or monogamous, birth control or radical politics, encountered a fierce hostility. It was a hostility fueled by the belief that such women and their views were corrosive of the marital, domestic ideal.

What made Victorian life a man's world was not only the power of this domestic ideal, but the simple demography of Victorian life. In England there was always a surplus of women. This had the effect of leaving one woman in three unmarried at any time; one in four never married. It was from among such women that the 'typical' Victorian 'spinsterish' professions developed: the governess, the teacher, the companion, the late-century clerks, secretaries, nurses and typists.

Sex before marriage was unusual. From the mid-eighteenth century onwards, demographers have discovered an increase in the rates of illegitimacy and bridal pregnancy. But it was still on a relatively small scale. Allowing for marked regional variations, illegitimacy rates were 6 per cent in the early nineteenth century, falling to 4–5 per cent late in the century. Something like two-fifths of brides were pregnant at marriage. Among people who lacked mechanical or artificial control over their own fertility, abstinence was preferable to the economic or social disasters of unwanted pregnancy.

This seemed to be less troublesome at the lowest reaches of Victorian life. The very poor appeared untroubled by the conventions of sexuality which their propertied peers held so dear. Charles Booth discovered the fact in London: 'With the lowest classes, premarital sexual relations are very common, perhaps even usual.' While it would be wrong to deny this, it would be equally misleading to take it at face value. Throughout Victorian society successive investigators had expressed concern about the sexuality of the lower orders. To Victorians keen to categorise by class or race, it was tempting to imagine that the poor and the working class were as different in their social behaviour as they were in all other aspects of life. They looked different, they seemed a race

'THE OUTCAST', RICHARD REDGRAVE, 1851

'The Awakening Conscience', Holman Hunt, 1853

apart: why should they not be sexually different? Once more, however, the origins of those differences are to be found not in the genetic features so beloved of late-Victorian scientists and social scientists, but in the circumstances of domestic and communal life. In the squalor or overcrowding of parts of plebeian life, it was impossible to emulate the ideals of bourgeois domesticity, just as it was impossible to emulate other ideals of their social betters.

There were epidemics of propertied concern about plebeian sexuality in the first phase of industrialisation in the 1830s and 1840s, and in the period of renewed concern about urban life in the 1880s and 1890s. It was the scrutiny of plebeian domestic and working lives which led directly to questions of their sexuality. What shocked observers was not simply that it differed from the bourgeois ideal but that it seemed more debased and unchristian than they could have imagined. It took the intuitive intelligence of Beatrice Webb to cut through the middle-class propaganda and to see sexuality among the poor in its determining social context:

> To put it bluntly sexual promiscuity, and even sexual perversion, are almost unavoidable among men and women of average character and intelligence crowded into the one-room tenement of slum areas.

It is revealing that she did not attempt to explain away sexuality in terms of individual character or intelligence. But even that high-powered Victorian woman could not bring herself to write about incest until 1926, and even then in a footnote in her autobiography:

> The fact that some of my workmates – young girls, who were in no way mentally defective; who were, on the contrary, just as keen-witted and generous-hearted as my own circle of friends – could chaff each other about having babies by their fathers and brothers, was a gruesome example of the effect of debased social environment on personal character and family life . . .

Charles Booth's researchers submitted similar evidence:

> Drink is fostered by bad houses . . .
> Crowded houses send men to the public house . . .
> Crowding is the main cause of drink and vice . . .
> Incest is common resulting from overcrowding.

Not surprisingly, Rowntree made similar comments on York.

> The difficulty, and all but impossibility, of maintaining conditions of decency and morality in overcrowded houses must not however be overlooked, and it must also be remembered that this difficulty is

> not confined to 'overcrowded' houses, but exists in all houses where
> there are boys and girls past childhood, and where there is no third
> bedroom.

After all, the bourgeois domestic ideal was itself dependent upon those material conditions of home comfort – a decent home, with plenty of room and the latest items of domestic equipment – which were denied the poorer groups. Notwithstanding the improvements in domestic working-class life, it was the wretchedness of so many urban dwellers, even at the end of the century, which explained the failure of so many to follow 'normal' sexual codes.

It was, of course, from among the poor that prostitutes were recruited. They haunted the streets and thoroughfares of cities small and large. Throughout the day and of course the night, they plied their trade in areas where they were highly visible. Again, in a society alleged to be ignorant of, or failing to recognise, sexuality, the ubiquitous presence of prostitutes in urban Britain reminds us of the contrary reality. It was extremely difficult to visit or shop in the centre of London or the city of York without being aware of prostitution. Indeed it was a matter of great and continuing complaint that prostitutes were inescapable on British streets.

Such complaints were reinforced at crucial moments by the public campaigns against venereal disease, or against the Contagious Diseases Act. Equally contentious were the political outcries over other matters specifically sexual; for example, about child prostitution, and about the age of consent, raised from 12 to 13 in 1871 and to 16 in 1885. In the fifty years to 1887, almost a quarter of the prostitutes in York were aged 18 or under. Girls barely into puberty were prostitutes in Liverpool and Birmingham. The questioning of prostitutes often revealed that a substantial proportion had been sexually exploited before the age of consent. Of course, the prevalence of venereal disease placed a premium on virgins or relatively inexperienced young girls, a fact which greatly encouraged the levels of child prostitution up to the 1880s.

Estimates of the number of Victorian prostitutes varied greatly. Even the police figures, alarmingly high as they were, almost certainly under-recorded the numbers involved. But, again, the figures varied enormously depending to a large extent on police policy. After 1885 there was an increase in prosecutions of sexual offences. In London in mid-century there may have been upwards of 50,000 prostitutes. All the evidence points to a fact which we might intuitively have guessed; that women were driven into

'AT THE DOUBTFUL BREEZE ALARMED', WILLIAM ETTY, 1845

'A FAVOURITE CUSTOM', LAWRENCE ALMA-TADEMA, 1909

prostitution by economic circumstances. It was not a job to which women aspired but to which they gravitated from desperation. What role we assign to prostitution within the broader framework is of course a different matter. Was it a consequence of those repressions and frigidities within the middle-class marriage, for which only extra-marital sex could provide an outlet (for men at least)? Or was it a reflection on the continuing wretchedness endured by so many urban dwellers? Is it likely, for instance, that prostitution would have been so ubiquitous had the material conditions of life been much better for the lower levels? Indeed, when material conditions did begin to improve at the turn of the century, the number of prostitutes was thought to have declined. If the argument at the heart of this book is correct – that the major Victorian social problems were rooted primarily in the conditions of urban life – it is surely there that we will find an answer to questions about Victorian prostitution. Its relation to the bourgeois family might be incidental and not very instructive.

Prostitution, like so many other public and private forms of Victorian sexuality, is generally ignored by those keen to revive memories and images of Victorian life. Better-remembered are those incidents, bizarre in retrospect, in which nudity and sexual issues called forth Victorian prudery in its most extreme and public form. The covering of nude sculpture, the denunciation of nudity in art, the veiling of sculptured genitals – these and similar acts of coy Victorian reticence are often viewed as typical. We need to ask if this is so. William Etty's nudes prompted *The Times*'s correspondent to warn him 'not to be seduced into a style which can gratify only the most vicious tastes'. Raphael's nudes could be endured, but 'nakedness without purity is offensive and indecent'. Etty's nudes were considered 'mere dirty flesh'. Such moralising was not peculiarly British but could be found in other European countries and in the United States. This did not however prevent the rapid proliferation of nudity in art. In fact nude sculpture was to be found not simply in galleries, museums or libraries, but also in the most public of places. In the words of Peter Gay:

> They decorated parks and fountains; they were a commanding presence in public buildings. They stood in niches, covered walls, spread across ceilings.

One was on display at the 1851 Great Exhibition. For a people supposed to be reluctant to contemplate nudity, Victorians sponsored an amazing amount of public nudity in art.

Nor was public nudity to be found merely in art. Until the development of cheap swimming costumes, and the introduction of by-laws regulating nudity on local beaches, nude bathing was common. One commentator remarked 'upon the almost heathen indecency of our sea-bathing places . . . In most places but Britain, male bathers are compelled to wear some sort of decent covering, such as short drawers . . . the present indecency is not diminished by the unblushing intrusiveness of some of the fair sex.' When the Rothschilds visited Scarborough in 1858 they found nudity 'in the full glare of day and sunshine, there is a complete absence of costume . . .' It was like 'the garden of Eden before the fall of man, and hundreds of ladies and gentlemen look on, while the bathers plunge in the foaming waters, or emerge from them'. The diaries of the Rev. Kilvert contain numerous such incidents. In the Isle of Wight, in June 1874, he wrote:

> In Shanklin one has to adopt the detestable custom of bathing in drawers. If ladies don't like to see men naked why don't they keep away from the sight?

At Torquay, another observer was shocked in 1888 to see 'a number of working men (it was Saturday afternoon) [who] whisked off their clothes at the wall on the beach and ran like savages to the water'. At Bournemouth the same man was appalled to see

> boys and lads disrobe, and appear to delight in disrobing, just as ladies pass. Indeed the practices at Bournemouth are peculiar. I have seen a woman morning after morning bring down two girls to undress and bathe from the sands, not on the women's side, but among the men.

This author remarked on the 'forwardness of women' in Bournemouth who,

> not content with gazing down from the cliffs above . . . they are passing by or near the bathers, and one morning I saw a tall young lady accompanied by a boy deliberately walk along, and back again, the whole beach just in front of a very long line of men drying or dressing themselves on the sands.

At Ramsgate, he noted the sea full of 'all sorts of little cockneys . . . sans gloves, sans well-brushed hat, sans slender silk umbrella, and sans almost anything'. At Southport, visitors complained of men 'shamefully exposing their person, to the great annoyance of females'.

Nude bathing was largely a male phenomenon, though it took the special interest of the Rev. Kilvert to capture female nudity on the beach.

> One beautiful girl stood entirely naked on the sand, and there she sat, half reclined sideways, leaning upon her elbow with her knee bent and her legs and feet partly drawn back and up, she was a model for a sculptor, there was a supple slender waist, the gentle dawn and tender swell of the bosom and budding breasts, the graceful roundness of the delicately beautiful limbs and above all the soft exquisite curves of the rosy dimpled bottom and broad white thighs.

Kilvert is an interesting case; he clearly looked hard and long at this particular young girl. But, for our purposes, it is important that she was seen, unashamedly naked, on a Victorian beach. Many Victorians were undoubtedly troubled by nude bathing, but its frequency is scarcely consonant with the received view that our nineteenth-century forebears were collectively obsessed with removing all traces of the naked body from public view. There was an undoubted drive against nudity in public, in artistic form or on beaches, in part by those who thought that such sights encouraged the 'lonely sin' of masturbation. But the successes of such campaigns pale into insignificance when set against the persistence, ubiquity and common acceptance of nudity in public places.

There were many Victorian responses to, or discussion of, sexual matters which provide the modern observer (almost certainly influenced in some way by a post-Freudian view of sexuality) with an easy target for ridicule or condemnation. Medical opinion about masturbation, and its alleged dire personal consequences; popular (and medical) views about the effects of menstruation; the sharp line of gender which was widely accepted as the immutable distinction between human abilities, potential and even mentalities; the sheer ignorance among Victorians about physiology and about sexuality, notably in its unconventional forms – all these and more create an image of Victorian life which seems utterly remote from our own. Yet there were aspects of Victorian sexuality which do not belong to this world of the unimaginably remote and unsympathetic past. On questions of sexuality, Victorians were frequently at odds with one another. They did not share a code of values which were unquestioningly accepted by all throughout the epoch. The Victorians were, by turns, both prudish and permissive. Any attempt, in retrospect, to suggest that Victorians can readily be herded into one moral camp is to do a gross injustice to the remarkable diversity of outlook, the conflict of opinions, the continuing arguments about moral issues, which permeated Victoria's reign.

II

OTHER PEOPLE,
OTHER VALUES

MANY of the 'Victorian values' which are well remembered and discussed today came to the fore in the last century to form part of a code of behaviour designed to govern every aspect of life. Some of the values perceived today as Victorian in origin – attachment to family, obedience to betters and thrift for example – are not Victorian at all, but trace their roots to much earlier periods. Often, they formed part of that broad Christian and legal tradition which has given distinctive shape to British life and institutions over many centuries. Nevertheless the Victorians often did feel the need to re-shape and re-formulate many of these older values, or to develop new ones, in order to cope with and make sense of the rapidly changing world around them.

We remember 'Victorian values' so well for a number of obvious reasons, not only from the lessons of elders who were themselves Victorians, but also because the Victorians were great moralisers and their words survive in greater profusion than from any earlier period. Victorian life came to be influenced by the printed word, thanks to the revolutions in printing and distribution, and to the development of mass literacy. In print, all sorts and conditions of Victorians could moralise and pontificate cheaply, on a scale and with a persistence previously unimagined. There were whole new categories of writers and public speakers whose words and ideals were instantly enshrined in printed form, to be sold or given away in the hope that their message, on behalf of some particular cause, would reach its chosen target. Philanthropic ladies addressed other ladies about the plight of their chosen beneficiaries, successful businessmen advanced their own formulas for success, clergymen pubished sermons and pieties by the ton, civic and national leaders vied for support by attaching themselves to this or that moral issue; an extraordinary literature was spawned.

But can we explain why Victorians moralised so much more than earlier generations? It was probably because they faced numerous serious problems, never previously experienced on such a scale, which were the concomitants of the new industrial and urban world. In addressing themselves to these problems, Victorians felt obliged to advocate certain values which offered solutions or escapes, strength where they saw weakness, virtue where they saw vice, and progress where they saw despair. As a rule the values they promoted reflected not the world as they saw it, the harsh social reality around them, but the world as they would have liked it to be.

More than that, however, the assiduous promotion of such values created a moral climate which provided an apparent explanation for Victorian economic and social success. In material terms, well-off Victorians were very well-off indeed. Their mature industrial economy dominated world markets by the late century; their empire grew ever more expansive. It was the most successful industry and empire the world had yet seen, though by the end of the period there were clear flaws in the edifice. It was easy to assume, then and now, that Victorian successes were intimately linked to those contemporary ideals which flowed so abundantly from the new presses into, it was hoped, the grubby hands of a newly literate and pliable British public. The massive literature available acted as gospel and guide to personal and collective conduct, finding its justification in the material achievements of the British people, at home and abroad. The reality of Victorian life however was more complex and often quite different.

Many 'Victorian values' were so frequently rehearsed in print not because they were the norm, or even because they were finding acceptance, but because, on the contrary, they were failing. Often as not, they were espoused by interested parties alarmed at the depredations they saw around them. Public exhortation of such values were thus attempts to cajole and persuade a resistant people to accord to those forms of behaviour which its advocates felt best for them. These values seemed to offer a solution to a particular problem or crisis. Organised religion, for example, was most passionately promoted when it had become clear that irreligion or apathy were on the rise. The virtues of family life were most vigorously advocated by those to whom the family was under siege. Industry and hard work were the gospel of those whose own self-interest was best served by it, but who also saw it as missing from others.

Advocates of so many of these Victorian values directed their proposals, of course, not so much to their peers but to those people thought to be most in need of them: working people. From the early days of urban and industrial change through to Victoria's death, and into our own century, working people were assailed on all fronts by the values promoted by their social betters. True, there was a parallel and reinforcing trend, of plebeian spokesmen advocating similar solutions; but most advice came from above, from pulpits, from the manager's office, from the Sunday school leaders and later from the school teachers.

Probably the most persistently advocated notion throughout the nineteenth century was the need to work hard. Again, there was nothing new in this. Clergy and property-owners had long been advocates of industry on the part of their flock. But the nature of work, and of attitudes to it, changed fundamentally with the development of modern industries and of a highly urbanised society. Yet in 1700 no less than in 1900 the attractions of hard work, for those who had to do it, were not so much its alleged satisfaction as the need of most working people to eke out a meagre living by its means.

The patterns and rhythms of work changed substantially in the course of the nineteenth century. As industry, the machine and the clock came to dominate more lives, the earlier work disciplines gave way to those familiar to modern eyes. It was a slow, uneven progress, fought initially by pioneering industrialists keen to discipline their labourers' work habits to the demands of machinery. In time the battle was joined by other important institutions and their spokesmen. Sunday schools and later the compulsory elementary schools placed great emphasis on punctuality and application. Diligence, good time-keeping and good behaviour were rewarded, normally by the gift of books. By the end of the century, institutions of all kinds rewarded a lifetime's activities of their older members by the gift of a watch or clock. Time measured out by the machine, not that dictated by the sun or the seasons, had come to impose a different and totally new discipline on the British people. For those with no timepiece of their own, major Victorian buildings were often topped by a clock; while industries had their own system of communal timekeeping, using hooters or a peripatetic 'knocker-up'.

Failure to keep 'good time' involved financial penalties; it became vital for working people to keep to the clock. Similarly, their commitment to hard work, whether measured out by task or by time, was a function of crude economic necessity. This was no less true of agricultural work. In many occupations throughout this period, the continuing dependence upon child labour is an indication of the inadequacies of earnings. As must be clear from the evidence throughout this book, a great deal of British poverty was a result of low wages. Working people sent out their children to work, or kept them at home to work, not from cruelty or indifference to their children, but because the extra pence earned by their offspring often meant the difference between survival and destitution.

Hard work was the basic fact of plebeian life, from childhood to old age, imposed by harsh necessity and not in cheerful pursuit of the ideal of self-improvement advocated by their betters. This begs the question of why Victorians felt the need to encourage hard work if it was, anyway, the natural lot of working people. In response we should look, firstly, at the advocates of hard work, from Josiah Wedgwood to Samuel Smiles; clearly they had a vested interest in their pleas. Secondly, Victorians firmly believed that they had cast the world anew, that their energies had created the wealth of the industrial world, as indeed they had. Furthermore there were enough examples of rags-to-riches to convince people that anyone could improve himself. In an age which believed in progress, it seemed natural to believe that material progress would emerge from hard work. For a small handful of people, the self-made, this had been unquestionably true. No less true, however, was the converse: that for millions of Victorians a lifetime's hard work petered out in the poverty of old age. Hard work on its own could not transmute inadequate wages into the stuff of self-improvement.

There was a further, more complicated dimension to the belief in hard work as the inevitable route to personal and collective salvation. Its proponents were, in essence, wedded to the belief that human behaviour had its roots in personal, not social, explanations. Social problems were thus a result of collective personal weaknesses and flaws and did not derive from failings in society itself. For those Victorians who viewed social problems in this way hard work seemed to offer an antidote to the major ills of individuals and therefore of society. This view of the world was totally at variance with the evidence from the great investigations into poverty in the last twenty years of the century, but it was an article of faith, an assumption about human nature, which could not readily be shaken, still less disproved by statistics. At the very

'INTERIOR OF A TEMPLE OF JUNIPER'

'WORK', FORD MADOX BROWN

'RAMSGATE SANDS', FRITH, 1854

end of our period after Rowntree's work had been published, Helen Bosanquet remained insistent that

> When all is said and done which well-wishers can say or do, it still remains true that the strength of the people lies in its own conscious efforts to face difficulties and overcome them.

This view of human nature persisted, alongside changing social policies and problems, right through the twentieth century.

It was easy to imagine that so many working people were struggling to survive only because of their inability to manage their finances and households adequately. Victorians lacked no shortage of advice on how to do this. Instructions on family budgeting, on how to devise the cheapest but adequate meals, on how to make clothing were plentiful throughout the century. Most of it was wasted, for very little even reached the people to whom it was addressed. This situation began to change markedly from 1880, when the schools were able to instruct girls in the business of household and housekeeping skills. But even then, it was often done in a form which was quite alien. Cooking utensils and foodstuffs were used which few of the girls from low income homes could ever hope to see, still less buy and use.

Formal instruction in thrifty, penny-wise household economy was directed at girls and women of all social classes. Books on household management and budgeting, including instructions on management of domestics, were important items in the education of young girls from the middle and upper classes. For the lower income groups, the lessons of economy, of living within one's means, needed no formal teaching. For much of the period, there were few material objects other than the necessities of life on which to spend spare cash, and spare cash was rarely available anyway. During the last quarter of Victoria's reign more material goods, both luxuries and essentials, came on the market, and increasing numbers of people had more spare cash to divert to these ends. It was in these years that many of the familiar Victorian household objects began to appear in working-class homes: the furnishings, pictures and pianos. Working people began to spend their spare money on a variety of new pleasures: on music halls, sporting events, trips to the seaside and other enjoyments. Yet all this new materialism of the late Victorian era could not mask the reality of life for the have-nots, the millions locked into wretched urban poverty. Rather, the emergence of new forms of plenty served simply to highlight their poverty. This sharp contrast is a feature of

British life in the late twentieth century no less than it was in the late nineteenth century.

Whether one perceived all this depended on one's social outlook. The belief in self-improvement through industry and thrift was so ingrained in many propertied Victorians that the continuing plight of the many in the midst of a prospering nation merely confirmed their view that personal weakness was responsible. There was evidence available which seemed at first glance to confirm their judgement. Many working-class people were indeed actively improving themselves. The money deposited in local penny savings banks came primarily from low income groups, often from domestic servants. The Post Office Savings Bank was established in 1861 for a similar purpose; by the 1890s it had almost six million savers, large numbers of them women and children. By the 1870s more than one and a quarter million members paid money into friendly societies, which were the acme of prudent, long-term thrift and economy. Indeed, at that time they had more members than the trades unions. And in the various and flourishing co-operative organisations there were clear signs of working-class material self-improvement through thrift, economy and self-help. All of these institutions, when linked to that profusion of learning facilities rooted in late-century working-class communities (which also spanned the century), provided ample evidence of a thriving plebeian commitment to the very virtues so many of their betters urged upon them. More often than not, however, these organisations were created by the upper reaches of the working class, the 'aristocrats of labour'. Membership and funds of these bodies increased markedly by the late century and their efforts at self-improvement were universally admired by all who knew them. Such self-help and material improvement served to wean working people away from radical politics. But what could be done for those troublesome layers of urban life which remained beyond the pale of self-improvement and immune to theories of thrift? It was not possible for a man on inadequate, or irregular, wages to be won over to the idea of thrift as a way of life.

Those convinced of the poor's moral shortcomings had only to point to the huge levels of drunkenness to strengthen their case that the poor failed to help themselves. Victorian moralists returned time and again, in print and in cartoons, to drunkenness and its effects in British cities. There was no doubt at all that pubs and other drinking places were heavily concentrated in poorer communities. The poorer the local district, the more pubs, and drunks, there were. Alcohol was consumed in vast – and until the 1870s, ever-increasing – volumes. In 1876 the average annual consumption of beer was 34.4 gallons. Although the vernacular phrase speaks of being 'as drunk as a Lord', it was plebeian drinking which alarmed the critics.

The available evidence certainly indicates that labouring people spent more on drink than they could objectively afford; but to put the situation this way is to misunderstand why so many of them drank such volumes. Booth and Rowntree in their surveys confirmed high levels of drinking, but was this a cause of the poverty they studied or its consequence? Throughout the Victorian period there was a fierce debate about licensing and restrictions. Sundays apart, pubs were open most of the day, and they were the permanent target of a persistent, but generally unsuccessful, band of temperance campaigners. When drinking began to decline from the mid-1870s, it did so as a result of those newer attractions which were now competing for working-class spare time and money. Even so, levels of excessive drinking remained high, as Booth and Rowntree confirmed, though not as high as many believed. For the poor, drink was an anaesthetic which blunted the miseries of their lives even if it made them poorer. Drink, not religion, was the opium of the masses. The attachment to excessive drinking would end not when the poor were convinced by the arguments of the temperance lobby, but when their material conditions were improved. In 1901 this remained an impossibly distant prospect for millions of town dwellers.

Vigorous efforts were made to lure people away from their troublesome habits, of which none were more troublesome than drink, by the deliberate creation of other attractions. 'Rational recreations' were provided by well-meaning local patrons in the hope that they could secure the allegiance of local working people. Local reading rooms and libraries, mechanics institutes with their lectures, classes and self-improvement, musical entertainments in local town halls and churches, were consciously used as alternatives to the more traditional pleasures of the working class. They were popular on their own terms but never successful in their aim of channelling the social energies of working people into more acceptable pursuits. Not until the gaudier delights of the late century arrived did plebeian pleasures begin to change, and only then primarily for men. What emerged – the commercial pleasures, seaside trips, football, music halls – often failed to come up to the standards which the propertied expected of their inferiors. What the ideologues of rational recreations wanted was good behaviour and personal improvement running hand in hand with enjoyment; leisure ought to be pleasurable yet elevating, entertaining but useful. It remained a source of great disappointment to those who tried to set a new tone among the nation's lower orders that they had failed persistently to implant an attachment to higher values, to dislodge those immediate and transient pleasures to which the common people remained resolutely wedded.

There are numerous other illustrations of the broader issue revealed here, some of them traced elsewhere in this book. The attempts to encourage thrift, hard work, sobriety or useful recreations form interesting stories in themselves, but they are elements in a much more significant argument so often misused, or ignored, by more recent proponents of 'Victorian values'. A great many of these values paraded in the 1980s as relevant to the condition of Britain in the late twentieth century were dependent upon the particular circumstances of life in Victorian Britain. We need to recognise that many of the 'values' were developed as a response to a contemporary problem or difficulty, not as the outcome of a prevailing Victorian strength or achievement. The advocacy of these values was generally the work of men and women worried about the nation's poorer people. True, many if not all of these values were of equal application to all strata of society. Indeed, many had been refined and given their essential Victorian form by the upper or, more often, the middle classes. There were then other values, perhaps the best-remembered Victorian values, which formed a creed of propertied life; principles of private and communal behaviour which seemed of universal application and value. They formed, in essence, an ideal code of life to which people of property consented and which they wished to see followed by all their compatriots. But it became necessary – notably at times of national crises and stress – to urge those values stridently and specifically on those legions of Britons whose lives seemed untouched by the aspirations of their betters. It was thus the problems of working-class urban life rather than its merits that gave rise to the propagation of 'Victorian values'.

This argument can, of course, be overstated. Those Victorians whose voices were loudest were proud of the achievements and the qualities of Victorian life and were unashamed to promote the virtues which, they felt, underpinned their nation's success. But they were, equally, alarmed at the manifest failures evident around them. And so often those failings seemed to find their strength and nourishment in the persistent wretchedness of millions of poor Victorians. They formed, in a sense, a collective problem; a problem which could only be solved by encouraging an attachment to those very virtues which seemed to be the nation's greatest strength and distinction. The continuing failure of the lower orders to accord to those virtues was inevitably matched by the continuing stress placed on those virtues by their betters. Yet how could people most in need of such values ever hope to acquire them when their domestic, communal and working lives offered them little but a cycle of unending wretchedness? What dim attraction could the persistent moral crusades of prosperous Victorians offer to millions of their compatriots who were different in almost every physical and social respect? Poor British people were smaller, weaker, shabbier, dirtier, more ignorant and smelled worse than their betters. What possible use or benefit, what possible attraction – save possibly for disgruntled envy – could the British poor hope to see in the moralising of their betters? It seemed but a matter of words, many of them incomprehensible. And to what avail were words when what those people needed was an improvement in their material lives?

VICTORIA
AND VICTORIANS

Any general study of nineteenth-century British life would be incomplete without some mention of the person who gave her name to the period. Queen Victoria reigned from 1837 to 1901; her life spanned most of the century and she witnessed the momentous changes which transformed her nation, people and empire. The difficulty of generalising about her life and reign illustrates the precise problem of generalising about the era; what was true of Victoria and Victorians in 1837 had changed by mid-century and was utterly transformed by 1901. Indeed this difficulty is perfectly illustrated by the story of the monarchy itself.

Victoria inherited a throne of dubious popularity, but bequeathed to her elderly son an institution which was strong, popular and apparently indispensible to British political life. Yet in the course of her reign, the monarchy had endured changing and sometimes mixed fortunes. The goodwill shown towards the young Queen gave way to a respect for the devotion to duty perfected by Victoria and her influential consort. Albert's death in 1861 left Victoria bereft. Emotionally distraught and personally isolated, she found strength during her unpopular period of widowhood in the flattering attentions of Disraeli and the unflinching loyalty of her Scottish servant John Brown. The low point in her personal life coincided with her nadir of popularity, but this in its turn gave way to a grudging and later a widespread national approval of an ageing monarch whose personal foibles and quirks were more than compensated for by her dedicated application to her position and people. Towards the end of her life Victoria had been transmuted from elderly monarch into a national symbol. Her name, image and iconography were emblazoned on statues, buildings and artefacts around the world; she gave her name to vast new regions of the globe and she reigned over an empire the likes of which not even the most powerful of Roman emperors had seen.

By the end of her reign, it was difficult to see where the reality of monarchy ended and where the mythology began. Indeed Victoria had become so ensnared in a web of popular, at times sycophantic, awe and admiration that the reality of the woman and of the monarchy had receded from view. Victoria personified all that the British had achieved, at home and abroad, in the course of her reign. Thus she offered her subjects the chance to reflect and take pride in those achievements. Her name and the adjective derived from it became the simplest way of capturing everything the British prided themselves in. The historian W. E. H. Lecky wrote, in 1908, that the Queen had been 'a moral force'. What Lecky and so many other Victorians admired in the Queen was that she displayed the very qualities which had, or so it seemed, made Britain so distinctive and successful. Victoria worked hard right up to her death. She was driven by a sense of duty and obligation which was exemplary. Victoria made this confession in her diary on 1 January 1881:

> I feel very anxious, and have no one to lean on. Thank God! My dear ones are all well . . . God spare all I most love, for many a year, and help me on! I feel how sadly deficient I am, and how over-sensitive and irritable, and how uncontrollable my temper is, when annoyed and hurt. But I am so overdone, so vexed, and in such distress about my country, that that must be my excuse. I will daily pray for God's help to improve.

Whatever her failings, no one could doubt Victoria's sense of duty. Although not a clever woman, her application and industry saw her grow into an immensely knowledgeable and experienced monarch whose opinions impressed her own and European statesmen. The Queen also overcame adversity to prevail in her work. She was, equally, a model for the proponents of family life, her state duties never obstructing her supervision of the rearing, and later the marriage, of her nine children. Perhaps her greatest achievement was the stability and strength which she gave to the monarchy.

To recite these qualities, however, is not to overlook the monarch's shortcomings. Often, when judged from the more democratic world of the late twentieth century, Victoria seems perverse and rigid. Equally, it would be absurd to expect a nineteenth-century monarch to espouse causes attractive to people a century later. She proved doggedly resistant to many of the ideas and proposals of her contemporaries. She clashed with her ministers over foreign affairs. When she disliked a policy she openly told the appropriate minister. She loathed Gladstone's proposal for Irish Home Rule and plotted to see it aborted. She sought to impose conditions on a new administration. Gladstone became a particular dislike and she scrutinised his various governments' actions with a hostile eye. Naturally enough, with so many of her children married to European royalty, the elderly Victoria played an open role in European affairs. Although earlier in the reign Victoria had been an admirer of, and was beholden to, Sir Robert Peel, she remained deeply hostile to Gladstone, the obvious heir to Peelite traditions in politics. Victoria was opposed to the idea of 'a democratic monarchy', hated radicalism and thought Joseph Chamberlain was a socialist. She was unsympathetic to extending women's rights, despite her own obvious personal example. She issued memoranda to ministers when she found herself in open disagreement with them. Although Victoria accepted that the respective power and positions of monarch and ministers were changing as the century advanced, and as politics were democratised by the Reform Acts of 1867 and 1884, she was in no way ready merely to assent in the judgements of her ministers. Victoria was no mere cypher, and the fact that her outspokenness and resistance were often directed against issues which many now might view as liberal measures, does not alter the point that the Queen had a political voice which she felt free to express. There were memorable incidents when Victoria disputed government policy, and it was not thought odd that she should do so. In the intervening years, the monarch has clearly been reduced in political voice.

These then were among the principal characteristics of the woman whose name has become synonomous with her era and with the *mores* of the time. But it is perfectly clear that in many respects she was not, and could not possibly be, typical or representative. She stood, alone for half her reign, at the apex of the British court and government, in contact with the rarefied world of courtiers and aristocracy, dealing with ministers primarily from landed and aristocratic backgrounds and sympathy. Deeply concerned for her subjects and keen to promote what she considered to be their best interests she was, inevitably, distant and removed from them, far more so in fact than the late twentieth-century monarchy.

From the beginning, she was dependent on the advice and encouragement of a small number of men. There were no suitable women to train her in the peculiar skills of being Queen, although she surrounded herself at first with the wives and daughters of

QUEEN VICTORIA AND PRINCE ALBERT, 1840

THE QUEEN AS A WIDOW, WITH BUST OF PRINCE ALBERT, 1864

ministers. Initially she turned to Lord Melbourne, who found himself greatly changed by the experience. He made efforts to curb his own swearing, but could do little to alter Victoria's imposition on the court of a new style of probity and good behaviour. The louche style of the Regency court gave way to the sterner air of the Victorian. In this, there is no doubt that Victoria's own sense of decorum and manners was crucial. Her marriage to Prince Albert in February 1840 confirmed the sober quality of court life. Never a popular man, he was nonetheless Victoria's greatest strength and undying personal passion.

If anyone was 'Victorian' it was Prince Albert. Serious, earnest, committed to industrial and economic progress, he was unsympathetic to British aristocratic ways. But he rode the tide of personal, often xenophobic dislike to impress himself on political and social life. More important, perhaps, his was the most influential voice on Victoria for twenty years, until his death in 1861. Both Albert and Victoria placed great trust in Peel, a trust which developed into friendship. Peel was, in Victoria's words, 'a great statesman, a man who thinks but little of party and never of himself'. Albert, unconsciously, shifted the attention of the court away from land and aristocracy towards the world of the new men of industry, business, and social reform. Victoria did not share these passions of her husband, but she revelled in his achievements, notably the Great Exhibition of 1851. Her own popularity was high, if judged by the crowds attending her periodic sallies, on the new railways, to visit provincial cities. Yet the popular press lauded her achievements not so much in statecraft but as wife and mother – though this may be rather more indicative of the values of provincial editors. Compared with the domestic disasters of earlier monarchs, Victoria's family life was indeed a triumph of Victorian domestic bliss. That ended, however, with Albert's death. Mid-Victorian Britain was led by a grieving monarch, scarcely able to contain her sorrow and reluctant to be seen in public.

It was at that time, in the 1860s, that party politics began to change. Ministers were now less willing to listen to royal advice, preferring instead to be led by the interests of party politics. And as Disraeli and Gladstone began to exert their political dominance, the relationship between monarchy and politicians as forged under Albert disappeared for ever. The Queen's insistence on duty survived, indeed strengthened; but for the last thirty years of her reign the monarch's formative political influence was eroded by the new structure of party politics.

Victoria was coaxed out of the depths of her mourning, which lasted effectively a decade, by Disraeli. She remained attached to the cult of her husband's memory, but slowly she was drawn back to a more normal pattern. Insistent upon her own inflexible annual routines, her time spent at Balmoral and the Isle of Wight, she also remained firm in expressing her own views about politics and statecraft. It was the image of a dutiful Queen, hard-working and solicitous for her subjects, which the press purveyed to the people in the last twenty-five years of the century. As with so many other areas of social history in those years, it is important to locate the monarchy in the context of an increasingly literate population, fed on a diet of print from popular newspapers and magazines, and educated in compulsory schools to place great value on the monarchy in general and Victoria in particular. Like love of country, affection for the Queen was high on the agenda of most of the press, and permeated formal lessons in schools. School books dealing with history and geography returned time and again to the glories of the monarchy and its symbolism.

> Beautiful England – on her island throne –
> Grandly she rules, with half the world her own.
> From her vast empire the sun ne'er departs:
> She reigns a Queen – Victoria, Queen of Hearts.

There were many objections to the newly-revived monarchy (enhanced with the title of Empress by Disraeli's Act of 1876); labour leaders and early socialists thoroughly disapproved, and Disraeli's opponents objected to his apparent hijacking of the institution. But such complaints were rare, and scarcely audible against a mounting chorus of monarchical praise and propaganda. As Victoria aged, she could do little wrong in the eyes of those most active in promoting her name and image among the British people.

In schools, the literature devoted specifically to the history of the monarchy had no trouble in elevating Victoria far above the average of earlier monarchs. They could point convincingly to the turmoil of 1837 and the general tranquillity at the end of her reign. One school book recorded that, at the accession,

> the land was filled with distress and unrest, and tens of thousands were suffering from want. But her people loved her and trusted her, and their love and trust was amply repaid.

Children's books stated boldly the affection felt for the Queen by the nation: 'So the English people love her now just as much as in

We don't want to fight, but, by Jingo, if we do,
We've got the ships, we've got the men, we've got the money, too.
We've fought the Bear before,
And while Britons shall be true
The Russians shall not have Constantinople.

DISRAELI OFFERING INDIA TO THE QUEEN, 1876

THE QUEEN AND THE MUNSHI, ONE OF HER INDIAN SECRETARIES, 1895

the beginning and still go on singing God Save the Queen.' It was assumed that the Queen's qualities affected her people. 'Her noble resolve to be good has helped to make her people good also.'

At the time of her death, Victoria had become revered, possibly more idolised than any monarch before. Yet the royalist euphoria of her last years, so closely bound up in the expansion of empire and, finally, the South African war, has served to mask earlier episodes in her reign which seemed uncharacteristic. It was forgotten that the imperial matriarch had once been an introverted widow, notwithstanding the understandable reasons for that mood. But this, in essence, is part of the problem in trying to summarise the mood, style and outlook of a reign which had spanned more than sixty years. No single characterisation could do justice to the development, the changes, the contradictions which marked the monarch and her reign. This is not to argue that she was inconsistent, for in many respects, for instance in her sense of duty to her office and people, she was the essence of consistency. But how could the young 'girl Queen' of eighteen have been similar to the old woman of eighty-two? The scarcely reformed Parliament of 1837 had become the recognisably modern political forum of 1901, dominated by modern parties. Victoria's subjects, primarily country people in 1837, were highly urbanised, and the most industrialised people in the world by her death. The social and economic unrest at her accession gave way to the general stability and tranquillity of the early twentieth century.

We nonetheless continue to use a simple term, Victorian, to describe a society which was utterly different at its ending from its inception. Of course it is one of the historian's most difficult, often clumsy, tasks to impose a sense of finite chronology on periods and events which do not readily lend themselves to such exercises. The task is apparently made easier when we deal with a monarch's reign; the chronology is organised for us. In the case of Victoria's reign, however, the remarkably long period raises its own problems, and historians, fastidious about change, have preferred to speak of early, mid- or late-Victorian society. To make our understanding of those years even more difficult, the term 'Victorian' has itself been subject to change in the twentieth century. At the end of Victoria's reign the term 'Victorian' was being used by younger people who 'were against all those things for which, so they felt, the Queen and her reign had stood'. This usage has persisted, growing more powerful and influential in the twentieth century. 'Victorian' became, and often remains, a derogatory term, used to dismiss a person, a thing, an idea, as outdated, old-fashioned or reactionary. Yet the attachment by many Victorians to quite opposite qualities was no less striking. Many were fierce supporters of 'progress', many felt that they had shaken off the shackles and constraints of earlier periods, and many were radical and reforming in a range of activities. The economic and physical achievements of the Victorian age would have been impossible had the Victorians been as reactionary and rigid as is often claimed.

Much of this image has derived from the social tone generated by certain quarters of Victorian life. The Queen and her court were perhaps the most influential purveyors of acceptable social norms, and there a rigid sense of decorum, propriety and even prudery were dominant. This did not however prevent the Prince of Wales, so aimless throughout much of his mother's long reign, from being a well-practised roué, the principal star in a *demi-monde* which was itself a rejection of virtually all 'Victorian values'. Nor did the court tone always influence senior statesmen. Gladstone, a formidable moralist himself, claimed that of the eleven Prime Ministers he had known, seven were adulterers. Nonetheless the court was influential in establishing codes of public behaviour which others, lower down the social scale, were expected to follow. It was in fact a widespread belief that influence in society at large came from above; that values, morals and behaviour were shaped by following the example of superiors. In 1895 *The Girls Home Companion* told its readers:

> each class of society has its own requirements; but it may be said that every class teaches the one immediately below it; and if the highest class be ignorant, uneducated, loving display, luxurious, and idle, the same spirit will prevail in humbler life.

Victorian writers were as anxious to call society's superiors to their moral stations, to set an example, as they were to urge the less fortunate to follow those examples. The court set a number of conventions to follow, few more tiresome, time-consuming or expensive than the elaborate rituals of bereavement and mourning; rituals which have left us with a rich and at times almost incomprehensible iconography of Victorian life. At the lowest levels of society however, such rituals were meaningless in the face of harsh economic necessity, though plebeian life was marked by its own set of mourning patterns.

What court and aristocracy did not do was to penetrate, to any degree, the social and political structures of provincial urban life. It was in the towns and cities of Britain that the middle class came to dominate the high ground of local politics and to exert a distinct social tone over their own communities. It was the middle class, the classic bourgeois, whose style, words and conventions most influenced urban provincial life. And it is that social tone, specific and particular as it was, which is best remembered as Victorian. It was the provincialism, the piety and the prudery of the local middle classes, federated through a chain of municipal authorities and business communities into a national force, which left its stamp on nineteenth-century life and which is often conjured forth to represent Victorian society. Non-conformist rather than Anglican, often 'vulgar' in their displays of new-won material wealth and possessions, attached to 'progress' in all things, limited in their own education but keen to send their sons to the reformed public schools, it was this group, varied as it was, which set the moral tone we think of as 'Victorian'. They exerted their own, largely philistine, influence over art and architecture, yet they were also responsible for building some of the finest of Victorian civic buildings and amassing remarkable art collections throughout provincial Britain. It was the same people who ringed their native cities with enormous homes, which they filled with heavy furnishings and elaborate fittings.

It was, however, upon their own communities that they sought to impress their distinctive tone and values. They were able to do this in part through the workplaces they owned or controlled. As we have seen, the workplace was an important setting for the encouragement of a number of new social skills and qualities. Similarly, they sought to educate their inferiors through the place of worship. But there were other means available to the ascendant middle class to impress their values and style on a local community. The local press was an obvious way to create public opinion; to encourage an increasingly literate people to follow the values beloved of the proprietor or editor. Moreover the prosperous middle classes created new institutions through which they hoped to stimulate a plebeian attachment to their own values. Libraries, reading rooms and other educational facilities were built to provide a focus for those working people, primarily men, keen to improve themselves through education. It was with a similar end in view that local manufacturers and entrepreneurs established an extraordinary array of musical activities for their workforce or local people. Bands, choirs, contests and recitals became a feature of urban life throughout Britain, all with the aim of entertaining and elevating the senses. It was hoped that music in all its forms would shift the popular attention away from the more basic, often cruder, enjoyments of earlier generations, turning instead to enjoyments which were more refined, more rational.

It was through their political control that such men were able to influence most directly the tone of their town. They could, as we have seen, encourage a sense of local civic pride, create a sense of awe in their own conduct of affairs through the costumes, rituals, parades and celebrations of local politics. These reached their apogée with the visit of royalty, aristocracy or a prominent national figure. But these were only the most colourful trappings of a political influence which affected everyday life. Local by-laws and regulations created a complex structure of civic amenities; but they also determined what could – or could not – be done. Parks and gardens were created, but they were subject to strict control and scrutiny; rowdiness and children's games, for instance, were generally prohibited. Detailed scrutiny developed of all forms of popular entertainments, and local licensing and controls began to curb what was deemed undesirable. Thus at seaside resorts (themselves, of course, major towns) nudity was restricted, then banned, beaches were segregated and beach entertainments severely controlled. Even the donkeys were licensed by the late century. Political elites exercised important control over the nature and direction of local policing through local watch committees and through directives from the bench. At their instance the police made their periodic purges of those activities the local middle classes disliked: excessive public drunkenness, intrusive prostitution, boisterous children on the streets. In the last years of the century police scrutiny turned towards a new problem, of youths and adolescents, those young men who had left school but had not yet been absorbed by family commitments.

It was possible, by the last twenty years of Victoria's reign, to regulate aspects of people's life to an unprecedented degree. But those governing the localities could never hope to be completely successful in imposing upon their communities the peaceable tone they sought. The autonomy, independence and variety of social life were all too strong, too deeply entrenched in plebeian life to succumb completely to the exhortations or the restrictions of their social superiors. Nor indeed did this tone meet with universal approval from all the middle classes. Throughout the mid- and late-Victorian years there was a critical chorus, notably from intellectual quarters, of the more abrasive, more obtrusive forms of Victorian morality, chiefly those purveyed by the self-made and the local politicians. In its wake came strident criticism of the 'new money', and of the vulgarity, philistinism and intolerance which it so often seemed to create. Dickens, Trollope, William Morris, John Ruskin, Carlyle, Matthew Arnold – all (and more) in their own way were severely critical of the social tone created by industrial life. 'Your middle class man', said Matthew Arnold, 'thinks it the highest pitch of development and civilisation when his letters are carried twelve times a day from Islington to Camberwell ... He thinks it is nothing that the trains only carry him from an illiberal, dismal life at Islington to an illiberal dismal life at Camberwell ...' There was, to be sure, snobbery in abundance here, but it provides an important reminder that the proponents of vulgar Victorianism were not without their contemporary foes among the educated elite.

The self-confidence, the moral certainties exuded by prominent local politicians and businessmen were only one element in a complex framework of Victorian ideas. It was, after all, an age riddled with doubts and disagreements, notably about religion and, increasingly, about the relationship between science and belief. Once more we are faced with a paradox, for although it is so often assumed that Victorians were strengthened by their convictions, were sure of their beliefs, to many of them their age was characterised by doubt and uncertainty. Looking back over the reign Frederic Harrison wrote, in 1911:

> It is an age of open questions – in theology, in morals, in politics, in economics. All the old foundations and buttresses of our institutions, our beliefs, and our future hopes have begun to sink.

Harrison sought to trace the consequences of 'the break-up of philosophical and religious certainties'. Even if we view this judgement extreme or partial, it nonetheless reflects a particular Victorian's view of the transformation in his lifetime. It may seem odd today that there are some who urge us to return to a system of values which many eminent Victorians themselves thought redundant, uncertain, or of dubious application. The simple truth of the matter is that it all depends on which Victorians the observer cares to emulate.

13
AN END TO
VICTORIAN VALUES?

VICTORIA'S death in 1901 was the occasion for a great deal of collective British self-analysis. By and large, contemporaries reflected contentedly on the extraordinary achievements and changes brought about in Victoria's lifetime. There seemed, at first glance, little reason to doubt the global ascendancy and the national self-confidence of the British people. In a world of major empires the British were the foremost of imperialists. Among industrial nations the British had been the pioneers and the inspiration. At home, the massive expansion of an urban population had been accompanied by the gradual establishment of social stability. This educated, stable, industrial and urban people seemed unique. Britain had avoided the bloodshed which had so recently afflicted France and the USA. Unlike Germany, Britain had not endured a struggle for national unity. Japan, though on the rise, was too distant and incomprehensible to be more than a curiosity. But more critical eyes, alerted by problems of the Boer War, saw serious flaws in this edifice of Britain's industrial and imperial power.

Life for the great majority of Victorians was much better, materially, than it had been for their parents and grandparents. But the wretchedness endured by many Britons continued to worry many people. The 'Two Nations' described by Disraeli, and profusely documented by successive social investigations, remained a feature of British life in 1901. Despite material improvement, despite philanthropic efforts and political changes, the poor remained inescapable in British life. What was it, then, about this society which should now seem so worthy of imitation?

The lure of the past does not of course always lie in its proven historical reality. Often its imagined and mythical qualities are even more attractive. In a Britain which is facing serious social and economic problems, the past represents a lost age of British superiority. For those keen to arrest British decline, Victorian Britain offers a seductive example. If the British people could be persuaded to adopt the values of their Victorian forebears, then perhaps the nation might re-establish its former pre-eminence. Such ideals owe a great deal to nostalgia, but little to economic reality.

In recent years historians have begun to pay serious attention to the question of nostalgia. In Britain today there is an extraordinary nostalgia for Victoriana. Where Victorian artefacts were, until quite recently, disliked and destroyed, they are now treasured and preserved. Victorian furniture, buildings, paintings and steam trains are just some of the more obvious objects which are lovingly preserved. This is but one aspect of a more broadly-based attachment to a fossilised and neutered past. This attachment has, in its turn, provided the basis for tourism, one of the nation's few growth industries. The tourist industry's emphasis on certain aspects of British history has led to claims that the nation might soon need a curator rather than a prime minister. In keeping with this nostalgic mood, in the 1980s Britain had a prime minister who sought to evoke memories of the Victorian past. Her evocation was not really of what had happened, but of those worthy and virtuous elements of the past which seemed attractive and relevant to contemporary life. The past was not so much revived as filleted, gutted and stripped of its unpleasant or useless bits, and served up as a tasty reminder of the good things we once enjoyed.

To many people Victorian life seems attractive when compared with the fierce problems of the present day. What offends many on the radical right of the Tory party, for instance, is the massive bureaucratic accumulation of twentieth-century Britain. In their eyes, the achievements of the past have been buried beneath an increasingly dominant modern state and its complex, intrusive bureaucracy. In the process those vital energies and spirit which once made the nation great have been obliterated. That the modern state is substantially a creation of the twentieth century, there is no doubt. Two world wars, two major phases of welfare legislation (1906–10 and 1945–51), created the state we know today. It is a state which, in seeking to safeguard and promote the well-being of everyone, 'from the cradle to the grave', is now blamed for many of the nation's shortcomings. In 1901 radical political opinion felt that only the state could solve Britain's major social problems. In the

1980s, the state has come to be viewed by many in the Tory party as the cause of many of those ills.

As early as 1968 Margaret Thatcher stated her views boldly:

> I believe that the great mistake of the last few years has been for the government to provide or to legislate for everything. Part of this policy has its roots in the plans for reconstruction in the post-war period when governments assumed all kinds of new obligations.

The feeling that the present day state has become a harmful force, alienating people and taking from them decisions which ought to be theirs, is not unique to politicians on the right. Opinion polls have confirmed the degree to which British people have come to distrust the British state and its agencies: the tax man, local authorities, national government, and the major nationalised industries. The most outspoken critics of the modern British state clearly belong to the right; but they speak with an authority based on an appreciation of broad public dislike of the modern British state.

The continuing debate about the state of the nation has itself proved divisive, as different interest groups seek to blame others, not themselves, for the nation's problems. Thus the electorate blames politicians, politicians blame each other, labour blames management and vice versa. The bureaucracy of the state, often in the form of its civil servants, is singled out for its crucial role in the whole affair. It is seductively easy to look back to better times, to a golden age before the slide into the complexities and inefficiencies of the modern state. Hence the attraction of the Victorian age. Then, or so it seems to some, life was simpler, uncluttered by a domineering state and Britain flourished as never before or since. The reality of Victorian life was much more complex. So too were the values which allegedly lay at the heart of Victorian life.

Many of those values long predated the nineteenth century. Close family life, for instance, was not a Victorian invention, though some Victorians promoted it more forcefully than their forebears. Similarly, thrift had long been a feature of British life, though it too was vigorously advocated by a new breed of Victorians. Other values had long been traditional features of British life: piety, chastity, hard work and obedience to superiors, for example. The traditional attraction of chastity was due more to the fear of pregnancy than to the promptings of the pious. Similarly, labouring people had, since time out of mind, been obliged to work hard and long. But they bent their backs from sheer necessity, not from the promptings of their betters. Love of country seems especially Victorian; but while Victorians may have given patriotism a new direction, it existed in the eighteenth no less than in the nineteenth century.

Some virtues were, it is true, peculiarly Victorian. Cleanliness was loudly proclaimed by many late Victorians, but it could not be adopted by whole layers of the British population because of the deprivations of domestic life. Moreover many of those values claimed to be Victorian were in fact much older than that. They were long-established mores and institutions of British life, though given a new dimension and stridency by Victorian apologists seeking to promote them for particular ends.

What then are we to make of the attempt to incorporate Victorian values into the philosophy of the modern Tory party? It is a new variation on an old theme; the attempt by politicians to monopolise history for their own political ends. But is Victorian life really suited to modern Tory interests?

Victorian life seems to offer useful political ammunition. The Victorian emphasis on individualism is attractive to modern observers keen to promote individual enterprise in modern Britain. This often takes the form of seeking to dismantle those state organisations which have emerged in the twentieth century, the foundations of which were often laid in the nineteenth century. This drive to privatise, to restore economic and social life to the golden age, is in fact a political move which can derive only partial and dubious support from the Victorian past.

Britain in 1901 had become a society in which the state intervened in people's lives in innumerable ways. Obviously the late Victorian state was utterly different from today's bureaucratic colossus. But it is wrong to imagine that Victorians were able, at the turn of the century, to conduct their lives untroubled by the agencies of the state and unhindered by legislation. One of the major transformations in the course of the nineteenth century was a tide of legislation and a creation of bureaucracies in all walks of life. At work, at home, at school, on the streets, and even when relaxing on holiday, Victorians were hemmed in by legislative restrictions and controls. Victorians had found it impossible to create their economic and social transformations without curtailing a number of earlier freedoms. The freedom of a minority to do as it wished had often to be curtailed for the betterment of the majority. It was a Benthamite formula, an attempt to balance individual self-interest with the greater good of society at large. In working conditions, education, health and urban facilities, the state had to create a protective legislative and administrative defence for people unable to protect themselves. Moreover it was these interventions by the state which enabled millions of Victorians to enjoy a better life than earlier generations. Supporters of untrammeled and unrestricted individualism continued to rail against the restrictions of the late Victorian state. But they were increasingly voices in the wilderness.

For those politicians keen to trade on the threadbare vocabulary and imagery of patriotism, it is salutary to recall the fate of the Union Jack. Once the symbol of British global superiority, it is now to be found draping the shoulders of football fans, stitched to a skinhead's jacket, or heralding a Loyalist or National Front march. Thus has the token of imperial greatness been transformed into a motif of the wilder fringes of contemporary British life.

The debate about Victorian values is, at heart, political and not historical, thus further compounding the historians' reluctance to discuss the matter. It seems odd that the British, so often blamed for their attachment to outdated practices and habits, should be asked to re-adopt values from the last century: odder still when it is also claimed that the nation's most serious problems originated in Victoria's reign. The Victorian values which survive are not Victorian at all but the long-established mores of the British people, principles, attitudes and institutions embedded deep in the make-up of British life over many centuries. They are in effect part of that broad cultural inheritance bequeathed from one generation to another. They are not the monopoly of a set of politicians; nor are they prized elements of a party's morality, to be dangled before the electorate at appropriate moments. Whatever else the evocation of Victorian values has achieved, it has highlighted, yet again, the extraordinary, diverse, and even bizarre visions of the past entertained by large numbers of people. This, after all, is perhaps one of the most seductive appeals of the study of history. One man's, or woman's, view of the past is just as good as another's – even when it is wrong.

SELECT BIBLIOGRAPHY

GENERAL

BARKER, P. (ed), *Founders of the Welfare State*, 1984.
BRIGGS, A., *The Age of Improvement*, 1959.
BRIGGS, A., *Victorian People*, 1971 edn.
KITSON CLARK, G., *The Making of Victorian England*, 1966 edn.
* EVANS, E. (ed.), *Social Policy, 1870–1914*, 1978.
* FRASER, D., *The Evolution of the British Welfare State*, 1980 edn.
PERKIN, H., *The Origins of Modern English Society, 1780–1880*, 1972 edn.
* READ, D., *England, 1868–1914*, 1979.
ROBBINS, K. G., *The Eclipse of a Great Power: Modern Britain, 1870–1975*, 1983.
* WALLER, P. J., *Town, City and Nation: England, 1850–1914*, Oxford 1983.
YOUNG, G. M., *Victorian England: Portrait of an Age*, 1936.

The books marked * are particularly useful and evidence from them is to be found in most of the subsequent chapters. The place of publication is London unless stated otherwise.

CHAPTER 1

COATES, D. and HILLARD, J. (eds.), *The Economic Decline of Modern Britain*, Brighton 1986.
COLLINGWOOD, R. G., *The Idea of History*, 1961 edn.
DELAHAYE, M., 'Victorian Values', *The Listener*, 2 June 1983.
LOWENTHAL, D., *The Past is a Foreign Country*, Cambridge 1985.
LUCAS, G., *The Historical Novel*, 1969 edn.
MARTIN, B., *A Sociology of Contemporary Cultural Change*, Oxford 1983.
MIDDLETON, P., 'For Victorian read Georgian', *Encounter*, July–August 1986.
'Victorian Values', *New Statesman*, Supplement, 27 May 1983.

CHAPTER 2

CHURCHILL, R. S., *Winston S. Churchill: The Young Statesman*, 1967.
FRASER, D. (ed.), *The New Poor Law in the Nineteenth Century*, 1976.
HAMISH FRASER, W., *The Coming of the Mass Market*, 1981.
KEATING, P. (ed.), *Into Unknown England*, 1976.
MATHIAS, P., *The First Industrial Nation*, 1983 edn.
ROSE, M.E., *The Relief of Poverty*, 1972.
RULE, JOHN, *The Labouring Class in Early Industrial England*, 1986.
SHEPPARD, F. K., *London, 1808–70. The Infernal Wen*, 1971.
TRANTER, N. L., *Population and Society, 1750–1940*, 1985.
TREBLE, J. H., *Urban Poverty in Britain*, 1979.
WALVIN, J., *English Urban Life, 1776–1851*, 1984.
WRIGLEY, E.A. and SCHOFIELD, R. S., *The Population History of England, 1541–1871; A Reconstruction*, 1981.

CHAPTER 3

BERRIDGE, V. *Opium and the People*, 1981.
BURNETT, J. *Plenty and Want: A Social History of Diet in England from 1815*, 1979.
CARTWRIGHT, F. F., *A Social History of Medicine*, 1977.
DUREY, M. J., *The Return of the Plague*, Dublin 1979.
FRASER, D., *The Evolution of the British Welfare State*, 1980.
ROWNTREE, S., *Poverty: A Study of Town Life*, 1901.
SMITH, F. B., *The People's Health, 1830–1910*, 1979.
WALVIN, J., *A Child's World: A Social History of English Childhood, 1800–1914*, 1982.

CHAPTER 4

BRIGGS, A., *Victorian Cities*, 1968 edn.
COLEMAN, B.I. (ed.), *The Idea of the City in the Nineteenth Century*, 1973.
DYOS, H.J. and WOLFF, M. (eds.), *The Victorian City*, 2 vols., 1973.
EVANS, E. J. (ed.), *Social Policy, 1830–1914*, 1978.
GAULDIE, E., *Cruel Habitations*, 1974.
GILBERT, A.D., *Religion and Society in Industrial England*, 1976.
GILLEY, S. and SWIFT, R. (eds.), *The Irish and the Victorian City*, 1985.
STEDMAN JONES, G., *Outcast London*, 1984 edn.
KEATING, P. (ed.), *Into Unknown England*, 1976.
KELLETT, J. R., *Railways and Victorian Cities*, 1979 edn.
ROBERTS, R., *The Classic Slum*, 1971.
WALLER, P. J., *Town, City and Nation: England 1850–1914*, 1983.

CHAPTER 5

BRIGGS, A., *Victorian Cities*, 1968 edn.
MITCHELL, R. J. and LEYS, M. D. R., *A History of London Life*, 1968.
SHEPPARD, F., *London 1808–1870: The Infernal Wen*, 1971.
SMITH, F. B., *The People's Health, 1830–1910*, 1979.
WALLER, P. J., *Town City and Nation, 1850–1914*, Oxford 1983.

CHAPTER 6

BAILEY, V. (ed.), *Policing and Punishment in Nineteenth-century Britain*, 1982.
COOPER, D. D., *The Lessons of the Scaffold*, 1974.
EMSLEY, C., *Policing and Its Context, 1750–1870*, 1983.
GATRELL, V. A. C., LENMAN, B, and PARKER, G. (eds.), *Crime and Law*, 1980.
IGNATIEF, M., *A Just Measure of Pain*, 1978.
JONES, D., *Crime, Protest, Community and Police in Nineteenth-century Britain*, 1982.
PHILIPS, D., *Crime and Authority in Victorian England*, 1977.
PRIESTLEY, P., *Victorian Prison Lives*, 1985.

CHAPTER 7

LAWSON J. and SILVER, H., *A Social History of Education in England*, 1973.
MACKENZIE, J. M. (ed.), *Imperialism and Popular Culture*, Manchester 1986.
MANGAN, A. and WALVIN, J., (eds.) *Manliness and Morality*, Manchester 1987.
PELLING, H., *Popular Politics and Society in Late Victorian Britain*, 1968.
PRICE, R., *An Imperial War and the British Working Class*, 1972.
VINCENT, D., *Bread, Knowledge and Freedom*, 1981.
WIENER, M., *English Culture and the Decline of the Industrial Spirit, 1850–1980*, Cambridge 1982.

CHAPTER 8

BRADLEY, I., *The Call to Seriousness*, 1976.
HARRISON, B., 'Philanthropy and the Victorians', *Victorian Studies*, 18, 1966.
HEASMAN, K., *Evangelicals in Action*, 1962.
MOWAT, C. L., *The Charity Organisation Society, 1869–1912*, 1961.
OWEN, D., *English Philanthropy 1660–1960*, 1964.
READ, D., *England, 1868–1914*, 1979.
ROBERTS, D., *The Victorian Origins of the British Welfare State*, 1963.

CHAPTER 9

CANNADINE, D., 'Civic Ritual and the Colchester Oyster Festival', *Past and Present*, No. 94, February 1982.

CUNNINGHAM, H., 'The Language of Patriotism, 1750–1919', *History Workshop*, No. 12, Autumn 1981.

FRASER, D., *Urban Politics in Victorian England*, Leicester 1976.

FRASER, D. (ed.), *A History of Modern Leeds*, Manchester 1981.

HENNOCK, E. P., *Fit and Proper Persons*, 1973.

KIERNAN, V. G., *The Lords of Human Kind*, 1969.

MALCOLMSON, R. W., *Popular Recreations in English Society, 1700–1890*, Cambridge 1973.

PORTER, B., *The Lion's Share*, 1975.

RANGER, T. and HOBSBAWM, E. J., (eds.), *The Invention of Tradition*, Cambridge, 1984.

RICH, P., *Race and Empire in British Politics*, Cambridge 1986.

WALVIN, J., *Passage to Britain*, 1984.

WRIGHTSON, K., *English Society, 1580–1680*, 1982.

CHAPTER 10

FINNEGAN, F., *Poverty and Prostitution*, Cambridge 1979.

GAY, P., *The Bourgeois Experience: Victorian to Freud*, vol. I: *Education of the Senses*, Oxford 1984.

GAY, P., vol. II: *The Tender Passion*, Oxford 1986.

HARRISON, F., *The Dark Angel*, 1981.

HIMMELFARB, G., *Marriage and Morals among the Victorians*, 1986.

JENKYNS, R., 'The Combustible Victorians', *TLS*, 8 August 1986.

Kilvert's Diary, 1977 edn.

MARCUS, S., *The Other Victorians*, New York 1967.

THOMAS, KEITH, 'The Double Standard', *Journal of the History of Ideas*, XX, 1959.

WALKEWITZ, J. R., *Prostitution and Victorian Society*, 1980.

WALVIN, J., *Beside the Seaside*, 1978.

WEBB, B., *My Apprenticeship*, 1971 edn.

WEEKS, J., *Sex, Politics and Society*, 1981.

WEEKS, J., *Sexuality and its Discontents*, 1985.

CHAPTER 11

BRIGGS, A., *Victorian People*, 1971 edn.

HARRISON, B., *Drink and the Victorians*, 1971.

ROBERTS, D., *Paternalism in Early Victorian England*, 1979.

THOMPSON, E. P., 'Time, Work Discipline and Industrial Capitalism', *Past and Present*, No. 38, 1967.

CHAPTER 12

BENSON A. C. and VISCOUNT ESHER (eds.), *The Letters of Queen Victoria*, 1907, 4 vols.

BLACK, E.C., *Victorian Culture and Society*, New York 1973.

BRIGGS, A., *Age of Improvement*, 1959.

YOUNG, G. M. and HANCOCK, W. D., (eds.), *English Historical Documents* XII(I), 1834–74, Oxford 1956.

HANCOCK, W. D. (ed.), *English Historical Documents* XII(2), 1874–1914, Oxford 1977.

LONGFORD, E., *Victoria RI*, 1964.

PICTURE ACKNOWLEDGEMENTS

1, 5, 7, 9, 11, 12, 20, 23, 28, 41: The Mansell Collection.

3, 16, 17, 18, 43: BBC Hulton Picture Library.

4: T. & R. Annan and Sons Ltd.

6: Manchester Polytechnic.

8: The Master and Fellows of Trinity College, Cambridge.

10, 21: Wellcome Institute Library, London.

13: Joseph Rowntree Memorial Trust.

14: Greater London Record Office.

19: National Portrait Gallery, London.

22, 24, 27, 33: Ann Ronan Picture Library.

29: Greater London Photo Library.

30: Eton College.

31: National Museum of Labour History, London.

34, 35: Salvation Army Archives.

36: Royal Academy of Arts, London.

37, 38, 39: The Tate Gallery, London.

40: City Art Gallery, Manchester.

42: Russel-Cotes Art Gallery and Museum, Bournemouth.

44: English Heritage, Historic Buildings and Monuments Commission for England.

46: By courtesy of Her Majesty the Queen.

INDEX

Britain(ish) – *contd*

habits of urban dirtiness 63; enjoys safer, stronger society through fresh water 66; decline in crimes against property and person 69; less crime in early 20th century 79; high standard of literacy in 94; pride in locality a feature of 108; development of sense of communal and civic attachment 111–12; role in world of major political importance in 1870s 114; patriotism due to firm belief in B. superiority 116, 117; doubts expressed by mid-Victorians about British 'national character' 117; foremost of imperialists 162; massive bureaucratic accumulation in 20th century 163; some virtues peculiarly Victorian in 165; society in 1901 165; legislation and creation of bureaucracies as one of many transformations in 19th century 165–6

Brown, John 148

budgeting and managing finances, plenitude of advice on 143

Burial Clubs 26

business groups, control of urban government by 112

by-laws and regulations, determination of what could and could not be done 160

Cabman's Shelter Fund 97

capital offences, reduction in number of 77–8

'Captain Swing' 69

Cardiff, expansion of 38

Cardwell, Edward, 114

Carlyle, Thomas 161; a severe critic of social tone creation 161

Catholicism, revival of 46

Chadwick, Sir Edwin 28, 36, 39, 56, 63: report on sanitary conditions of labouring people 28; report emphasising different mortality rates between classes in same town 34–5; his conclusions after studying water supplies 53; stresses economic cost of permitting urban filth to continue unchecked 63; works *Report on the*

Sanitary Condition of the Labouring Population of Great Britain (1842) 39q.

Chamberlain, Joseph 42, 51, 57, 65, 112: theory regarding regulation of monopolies 65; cited as politician seeking to inculcate civic pride and make city responsive to inhabitants' needs 112

charities(y), dislike of proliferation of 103

Charity Organisation Society: founding of 103; objects of 103

Chartism 22, 67, 69, 104

child labour, exploitation of 16, 27

children: deaths from whooping cough, measles, scarlet fever and tuberculosis 26; effects on caused by appalling working conditions 27; high proportion with defective hearing 27; alarm expressed by medical and social investigators at physical state of 27

cholera epidemics 1832, 1849 29

Church of England: building of new churches by 46–7; involvement in educational changes 85

Churchill, Randolph 66

Churchill, Winston 15, 23; appalled at Rowntree's survey of study of poverty in York 15

cities, difference between 55–6

city-centre shop 47

city fathers, expressions of pride in community 112–13

city life, as cause of many of Britain's physical problems 25

Clacton, contaminated water in 56

Colchester 'oyster feast' 111

collectivism: as only way of coping with Britain's urban problems 36; opponents of 37

conscripts and volunteers, work undertaken to clean up British towns 63–4

Conservative Party, development of constituency organisations 105

Contagious Diseases Acts 123

contagious diseases, total of deaths due to 28

conurbation: concept of 8; synonymous with dirt, disease,

Labour Party 1; creation of 105
labouring life, problems of 15–16
Lancet 30
law and order, reason for acceptance of 79
Lecky, W. H. 149; his admiration for Queen Victoria 149
Leeds: as one of largest towns in England and Wales 12; 'back-to-back' houses in 39; foulness of streets in 56
lesbianism, term invented in 19th century 121
Liberal Party, development of constituency organisations 105
libraries, popularity of 83
life style, shift from early to late Victorian 14
Liverpool, as one of largest towns in England and Wales 12
Lloyd George, David 24
local authorities, reluctance of to build homes for working people 41–2
Loch, S. S., leader of Charity Organisation Society 103
London: high rents in 40; worsening problems of housing in 41; problem of water supply in 54; its smells unrivalled 54; major problems of law and order in 67

Manchester, one of largest towns in England and Wales 12
Manchester Guardian 104
Margate, contamination of water in 56
Marshall, Alfred 51; views on state intervention 51
Masterman, C. F. G. 40, 52; works *From the Abyss* 40q.
Martineau, Harriet 100
Maurice, Major-General Sir Frederick 23–4; remarks regarding unfitness of volunteers for service in Boer War 23–4
Mayhew, Henry 22–3; works *London Labour and the London Poor* 22q.
Mearn, 105; works *The Bitter Cry of Outcast London* (1883) 105q.
medicine: improvements in 26; revolutionisation of 29–30; no clear dividing line between traditional and folk 30, 33

Melbourne, Lord 153; his association with Queen Victoria 153
memory, links with history 2
Merthyr Tydfil, described as being in sad state of neglect 56
Methodism, growth of 46
Metropolitan Drinking Fountain Association 97
Metropolitan Police, constitution of 69–70
middle classes: domination of local politics and influence on urban political life 159–60; creation of new institutions by 159
middle and upper classes, number of 17
migration in British Isles and overseas 13, 109–10
Mill, John Stuart 124; asserts middle-class family key to refinement of manners 124
millionaires, increase in number of 17
monarchy and politicians: disappearance of relationship between 153; disapproval of newly-revived monarchy by labour and socialists 154
Morant Bay revolt 1865 116
More, Hannah: initiator of Sunday schools 85; urges women to be philanthropic 99–100
Morris, William 161; a severe critic of social tone creation 161
mortality: infant and child 26; fall in rate of 37
municipal bath and wash house 61
municipal housing schemes, mooting of 42

nation, continuing debate regarding state of 164
Newcastle, a major 'provincial capital' 8
'new money' strident criticism of 161
newspapers and publications 81: proliferation of 81; flourishing of 82–3; sexual matters freely discussed in 123
Nightingale, Florence 30; works *Notes on Nursing* 30q.
Northcote, Stafford 36
Norwich, a major 'provincial capital' 8

encouragement of small number of men 150, 153; firmness in expressing views on politics and statecraft 154; idolisation and reverence towards 157; her essence of consistency 157; V. and court influential purveyors of acceptable social norms 158

Victorian(s): changes in way of life experienced by late 14; reluctance to spend money on home building and improvements for poor 41; accustomed to working in large buildings 51; penal policy of 77; late V. peaceable and law-abiding 79; pride in national achievements and imperial glory 94; generosity of in work for charity 96; charity focused on every kind of poverty 99; speculation on motives for philanthropy 99; their pride in town and country 108; regret at erosion and death of community-based popular culture 109; sexual attitudes and behaviour of 121; ignorance of sex by great majority of men and women 125; as great moralisers 137–8; reasons for moralising 138; belief in self-improvement through industry and thrift ingrained in 144; pride in achievements and qualities of life 146; a different society from inception to ending 157; use of term 'Victorian' as being derogatory 157–8; assumption V. strengthened by convictions 161; improved life of after Queen Victoria's death 162; emphasis on individualism 165; legislation and controls a major transformation 165

'Victorian values' 3–6, 137, 164: development of in response to contemporary problem or difficulty 146; formation of as ideal code 146; conclusions of attempts to incorporate V. values into philosophy of Tory Party 165; debate regarding values political not historical 166; views as to achievements of V. values 166

Victoriana, nostalgia for 163

virtues, cleanliness as Victorian 165

wages, huge rise in 14

water: as key to most important improvements in town life 53; evidence of close association between foul w. and endemic diseases 53; objections to provision of w. for whole country 57–8; increased demand for 61; imperfections in provision of w. and sewage 61–2; availability of fresh w. 63

water-carts, selling of water from 57

water-stealing 57

water supplies: remarkable improvements in 61; worst examples of poor supplies and sewage in rural communities 62

Webb, Beatrice 129: observations regarding sexual promiscuity and perversion among men and women of average character 129; observations on incest 129

Wedgwood, Josiah 140; an advocate of hard work 140

Weekes, Jeffrey 121; asserts Victorian life characterised by conflicts between contrasting beliefs and behaviour 121

Wesley, John 58; immortalises idea cleanliness next to godliness 58

Westminster Review 45, 103

Weston-super-Mare, contamination of water in 56

Wilberforce, William 100

Wilson, James 100

workhouses, building of 47–8

working-class youths and men in army, necessity not patriotism reason for joining 115

Work(ing) hard: persistent notion for need to 139; changing rhythms and patterns 139; hard w. as basic fact of life 140; salvation as reward for hard work 140

working people: benefits of 15; reluctance to attend church 47; Victorian values urged on 139; spare money spent on variety of new pleasures 143; depositing money in penny savings banks by 144; moralising by betters on virtues 147

working week, extreme length of 16